Palgrave Texts in Counselling and Psychotherapy

Series Editors

Arlene Vetere
Family Therapy and Systemic Practice
VID Specialized University
Oslo, UK

Rudi Dallos
Clinical Psychology
Plymouth University
Plymouth, UK

This series introduces readers to the theory and practice of counselling and psychotherapy across a wide range of topical issues. Ideal for both trainees and practitioners, the books will appeal to anyone wishing to use counselling and psychotherapeutic skills and will be particularly relevant to workers in health, education, social work and related settings. The books in this series emphasise an integrative orientation weaving together a variety of models including, psychodynamic, attachment, trauma, narrative and systemic ideas. The books are written in an accessible and readable style with a focus on practice. Each text offers theoretical background and guidance for practice, with creative use of clinical examples.

Arlene Vetere, Professor of Family Therapy and Systemic Practice at VID Specialized University, Oslo, Norway.

Rudi Dallos, Emeritus Professor, Dept. of Clinical Psychology, University of Plymouth, UK.

Åse Holmberg • Per Jensen

Working with Spirituality in Family Systemic Practice

Including Clients' Spiritual Life in Therapeutic Work

Åse Holmberg
VID Specialized University
Oslo, Norway

Per Jensen
VID Specialized University
Oslo, Norway

ISSN 2662-9127   ISSN 2662-9135   (electronic)
Palgrave Texts in Counselling and Psychotherapy
ISBN 978-3-031-77309-9   ISBN 978-3-031-77310-5   (eBook)
https://doi.org/10.1007/978-3-031-77310-5

This Palgrave Macmillan imprint is published by the registered company Springer Nature Switzerland AG.
The registered company address is: Gewerbestrasse 11, 6330 Cham, Switzerland

If disposing of this product, please recycle the paper.

The book has been revised. An acknowledgement section has been included.

ACKNOWLEDGEMENTS

Over ten years have passed since we began working together on the topic of this book—Åse, as a research fellow, and Per, as her supervisor. It has been an exciting, educational and interesting journey for both of us, and it is a pleasure that this has resulted in a joint book.

First, we would like to thank all the study informants, professionals and clients, who have freely shared their experiences on the subject. We have learned a lot from you.

Most of all, we thank Arlene Vetere. She has been reading and commenting and brought in suggestions that has been helpful all the way. Without her, no book.

We would also like to thank Arlene and Rudi Dallos for wanting to include this contribution in this book series.

Thanks also to the publisher Palgrave Macmillan, led by Paul Smith Jesudas and Liam Iscoe-Jones, who believed in us and who have been patient and supportive.

We hope the book will be a source of inspiration for practitioners in various systemic fields.

Contents

LIST OF FIGURES

PART I

Into the Topic

CHAPTER 1

Introduction

The mind is like a parachute.
It works best when it is open.
—Dalai Lama

If we look at our world today, there seem to be at least three perspectives we need more than ever: wisdom, peace and love. There is something deeply existential that forces itself forward, something which in many ways is in short supply in our Western societies. Economic development creates huge differences between people, while nature suffers from our overconsumption. Abuse of power and wars are just around the corner, and many young people lack faith in the future.

We can get almost everything online. It is easy to feel helpless and overwhelmed. This also applies to our clients who come for therapy. They are young, middle-aged or older, part of communities and the world at large. Many struggle to find a way—a meaningful life.

Some people seem to have little contact with their souls and their inner life. Deeper existential themes and restlessness might affect relationships, family and work in different ways. In a systemic world, everything will affect everything, to varying degrees.

Å. Holmberg, P. Jensen, *Working with Spirituality in Family Systemic Practice*, Palgrave Texts in Counselling and Psychotherapy, https://doi.org/10.1007/978-3-031-77310-5_1

So how do we help our clients to create resilience, so that they can stand more firmly within themselves. In other words, what do we have to hold on to against all destructive forces in our world, even if life does not turn out the way we thought and hoped for? Without a certain ability to let go and to find new trust, we will be unable to move on. How do we help people to feel liberated, raise their gaze and feel solidarity with and universal responsibility for the whole? (Rohr 2021).

This is where spirituality comes in. A biopsychosocial perspective is not enough to meet these challenges. We need to integrate the spiritual, existential side of being human as part of systemic therapeutic work. This book will therefore devote attention to our spirituality, how it can develop and grow, both for therapists and for clients, and how it can be integrated into therapeutic work.

Who Is This Book For?

Perhaps you immediately think: this is not a book for me. I am not interested in spirituality, religion or deeper existential perspectives. Others perhaps receive the book with interest and curiosity; this is a perspective I have missed in the field.

Our message is that regardless of whether you as therapists say you are religious, atheist, agnostic or whatever you want to call yourself, the book's theme is important. This is because, as therapists, we should be prepared to meet and include clients' spiritual lives in our practice. For many, spirituality is part of life. As systemic therapists, we should not think that the client only can get help with the spiritual part in the church or the mosque. In addition, many do not define themselves as religious but are still spiritual. How to find a room to talk about it?

As we show in this book, spirituality is a broader perspective than religion. We argue that spirituality is a part of life, even if we are aware of this to a greater or lesser extent. We also know that humans' spiritual life can look very different, based on culture, traditions, experiences and context.

This is also about language. Our experience is that this topic arouses many emotions, often based on experiences that may not always have been as good. We also see that many people deconstruct and reconstruct their beliefs and views of life. What they have grown up with feels old-fashioned, uninspired and far too narrow-minded in today`s society. However, everything is connected to everything. Clients' spiritual life can be an important resource in therapeutic work. At the same time, we know that spirituality can create major challenges and be an underlying problem.

This book is written from our perspective as systemic therapists and researchers from Norway. We will elaborate on this in a later section. However, we hope the text can be an inspiration for the readers, and be a help to include spirituality in clinical practice.

SPIRITUALITY: HOW WE SEE IT

Spirituality is a concept that has many different meanings wrapped in culture, traditions and our various experiences. Spirituality comes from the word spirit, which means "breath", our "power of life". And this power of life is essential for being human. There can be many different words in the "spirituality box", such as soul, meaning of life, life philosophy, religion, faith and sacred, transcendent or existential perspectives. Even though these aspects of human beings can be very important in private life, they have a long tradition of being left out in health and social work, including in therapy (Holmberg et al. 2021; Walsh 2009b). In mental health, these topics have been pathologized and seen as part of a diagnosis. A positive curiosity and an acknowledgement that spirituality can be vital to cope with life have been absent (Holm et al. 2023).

We believe most people are on a spiritual journey, consciously or unconsciously. We know that if our biological breathing stops, we will immediately die. The body does not survive without the heart beating and the blood flowing in our veins. To be alive is about being present in ourselves and with others. To meet our self and others in love. It is about a connection to the living world where we are constantly becoming—in a process. We believe our spiritual journey is shaped by our yearnings. Our yearnings can lead us to deeper authenticity and integrity, and help us to be in motion. This is a way of living, bigger than a belief and a practice. Then we are part of something bigger, which is also a self-transcendence perspective. We need to ask: What makes life worth living? What makes you feel alive? What gives you meaning?

All spirituality is not healthy. What we call a "problematic form of spirituality" distances us from "life", and distances us from our body, emotions and innermost longings. It can block growth and development and make us egocentric, grandiose, insensitive and inhumane (Benner 2011). As humans, we need each other. My life is connected to your life. We believe our world needs more than ever, people who promote love, joy, peace, forbearance, kindness, goodness, faithfulness and humility.

To sum up: What can the spiritual mean to us?

The spiritual philosopher Sharon Janis (2008) states that despite life's various circumstances, a sense of the spiritual gives us the exhilaration of being alive. It can lead to a feeling of oneness with all things, which also creates a responsibility for life and the living. We are never alone in the world, and whatever we meet on our life's journey can be a deep lesson for our soul. The waves in life can be met with acceptance and detachment; they can give us a peace that can be difficult to understand with a rational mind. Co-creating life with a universal spirit can provide a great sense of power, where we are part of something bigger. This creates joy and is an inspiration for inner growth. It can give a state of peacefulness, contentment and self-acceptance, where we do not need to hide who we are.

LIFE IS A MYSTERY

Our being and our life can be understood as a mystery. There is so much we do not understand with our rational minds. Science cannot provide us with all the answers, and we will never be able to fully understand the nature of reality. We know that science has made great strides to save humanity, but at the same time, it has made the world infinitely more dangerous. A rational perspective is not enough. Nature is complex. The sum of the parts is not the same as the whole. The Irish neuroscience researcher, philosopher and psychiatrist McGilchrist (2021) has said: "The more important something is, the harder is it to grasp in language" (p. 1197). Therefore, we think we need to ask questions and have a wondering mind. There is always more than we have words for. Deep intuition can flourish only when not knowing provides us with enough space. A wondering mind creates new wondering.

Everything that exists is growing and becoming in relationships. Therefore, we have to accept uncertainty, that knowledge is limited. We believe we may tolerate ambiguity and paradoxes and be in the process of becoming. That means we have to get in touch with our emotional depths. Spirit, soul and physical body are different aspects of the same body. It is a question of experience, sometimes beyond words and reason. McGilchrist states that human spirituality is deeply loving. If we open us to love, it will do something to us. Love is a relationship, a movement towards another (McGilchrist 2021).

What is behind philosophy and science? Here we can only wonder. Nobody knows. But many have experienced a transcendent reality and believe that the invisible world is much bigger than the visible world (Drinkwater et al. 2021). Spiritual experiences may be non-intellectual experiences and can be referred to as mystical experiences. These can be experiences beyond words, accompanied by awe, wonder and humility. Everything cannot be measured and weighed or understood with our rational gaze. Life is a mystery, and a deep ocean to discover.

THE IMPORTANCE OF SPIRITUALITY

There are a large number of studies that tell us something about the importance of spirituality for human beings. We will limit ourselves to a cross-sectional survey from 2023 about spiritual needs among the Danish population (Stripp et al. 2023). This was the first large-scale study to examine spiritual needs in Danish culture and the largest study on spiritual needs to date. Surprisingly for the researchers, four out of five people reported that in the past month they had felt a spiritual longing or an existential need to find inner peace. From other spiritual needs came the need to do something for others. Being able to help to make a difference in the world. There was further the need to find meaning in life, or to forgive or be forgiven. Finally came what we can call religious needs, such as praying with someone, or being prayed for. This study demonstrated that spiritual needs are common among Danes. The researchers argue that Danish society turns out to be post-secular, so that faith and knowledge live side by side. To put it another way, despite the rise of secularization, religion is not dead. However, even if many people do not define themselves as religious, they are still spiritual. People get their sources of spirituality from many different places. However, the researchers believe that there seems to be an acknowledgement that there is something in life that is missing, a dimension, a strength in being human that many long for. A source of life inspiration and meaning.

From a systemic point of view, we are affected not only by our families but also by what happens in other relationships, in our environment and society at large. In our time, the threats to humanity seem to be increasing; we are surrounded by wars "close to home", pandemics, hunger, suffering and environmental disturbances. All the misery comes straight into our living room through our television set. This can make people uncertain about life and the future. Even if we are not affected directly, we are all reminded of the problems through the media and in conversations with others. However, death and suffering are a part of life for all. We are all vulnerable to different degrees, at different times in life. As family therapists, we meet people in difficult life situations, in various crises, when we cannot cope with life. Here, our spirituality can be a help and support, a lifeline in the midst of a storm, something to hold on to, a way to find direction in chaos (Holmberg and Jensen 2024).

Having an ecological perspective in life and practice means as we see it, being open to all aspects of humanity. Being open to the spiritual makes us more human. Despite this, people's spirituality is not always perceived as health-promoting. Sometimes downright harmful. We will go into this in more detail in Chap. 2, where we will deepen the spiritual perspective.

A SYSTEMIC VIEW OF SPIRITUALITY

The family therapy field has been silent about spirituality. Throughout the almost 75 years of its history, it is only quite recently that this issue has been highlighted more clearly. There have been a few bold scattered attempts in the past, as we will show in the next chapter, but none have had any impact.

Despite the systemic paradigm shift, we still carry with us the legacy of Freud, where religion and our relation to God were described as restricting freedom and immature (Danbolt 2014). We know that people can have different experiences of religion; it can limit their freedom and oppress them. Confusion about spirituality and religion can make people believe that they mean the same thing. A lot of therapists seem to have had bad experiences with religion and unfortunately they may tend to "throw the baby out with the bathwater". At the same time, 85% of the world's population call themselves religious, and religion can have great significance for people's life and health: https://worldpopulationreview.com/country-rankings/religion-by-country.

In addition, distinguishing between body and soul has set science against spirituality. It has resulted in a split between religion and science, where natural knowledge has belonged to science and supernatural knowledge has belonged to religion. Religion has been explained as the opposite of science (Adams 1995). Psychology, which originally meant "knowledge from the soul", has been "reduced to" science about the mind (Barker and Scammell 2016).

In our study, which forms the basis for this book, the informants felt a great deal of resistance to including spirituality in systemic therapy (Holmberg 2018). The therapists' reflections were that it was not interesting, embarrassing, too private, while several had no experience or knowledge of spirituality. They found the topic unworthy of reflection; they felt uncertain about it and had no time. Further, they felt that it was taboo in the field, a non-issue, not even politically correct. One said that it was outside the mandate of his family therapy centre, a topic for people with special interests. These are interesting findings because they tell us something about the place of the spiritual person in systemic therapy. However, as we will see, many therapists also include spiritual perspectives in therapy, and both therapists and clients made reflections on how this could be done appropriately.

In any case, to be systemic is for us to naturally adopt a spiritual focus. The British social anthropologist and systems and communication theorist Gregory Bateson (2000) encouraged us to look beyond the self and contemplate the "pattern which connects". A systemic view of life is a holistic view of life, where people's spiritual life is also part of the whole (Holmberg and Karlsson 2023).

Systemic therapy and thinking are based on philosophical and humanistic practice. Humanity refers to compassion and care for people, groups and societies who are struggling to cope, with a way of life characterized by compassion, tolerance, respect and democracy (Aadnanes 2012). Our self is not an individual identity; we are part of an ecological community, where we have responsibility for each other. Human beings create meaning and have value in themselves. Bateson (1979) referred to an ecological sacred world, where the relationship is the smallest unit. A systemic approach focuses on context and relationships. Human beings are part of many systems, which extend far beyond the therapy room. This also includes a relationship to something greater than oneself, something divine, nature or a community.

How to work systemically has been the subject of much discussion. New theories and methods have emerged during the relatively short history of family therapy practice. The field has constantly been in development to better meet clients' various challenges. Both research and professional and client experiences form the basis for knowledge-based practice. To work systemically is not to adopt one particular method or technique but to work creatively in a complex reality to try to help the unique person sitting in front of us. Problems and events are part of contexts and expand our perspective on people and problems. We each construct our own understanding of the world and how we communicate will therefore be decisive for our well-being, growth and development. Systemic therapy is a relational dialogical process to help human beings with their feelings, attitudes and ways of being, so that they can live better relational lives. We want them to take care of their life and use their resources in a life-giving and meaningful way.

ENCOUNTERS WITH CLIENTS

When clients enter the therapy room, there can be many reasons to ask questions about existence or the meaning of life. As the family therapist Glenn Larner (2017) says: "Every systemic conversation can evoke something of the spiritual; the question is whether we are open to and listen for it" (p. 125).

From a systemic point of view, everything is connected, and this holds true no matter what kind of epistemology and spiritual framework clients may lean on. In encounters with clients, systemic practice is concerned with important values such as curiosity, empathy, client participation, and creating a safe and trusting relationship. Here we think it is also important to give space to the spiritual client.

As human beings, we are affected not only by our immediate family but also by what happens in our relationships, environment and society at large. We live in a time of great global challenges, and pandemics, war, hunger, suffering and environmental disturbances can make people uncertain about life and the future (Holmberg and Jensen 2024). Many can struggle to find direction or meaning in life and are concerned with the big existential questions.

Froma Walsh (1999), the editor of *Spiritual Resources in Family Therapy* says:

> *Most people who come for therapeutic help today are seeking more than symptom reduction, problem-solving, or communication skills; they yearn for greater meaning and deeper connections with others in their lives. Many are in spiritual distress at the core of physical, emotional, and relational problems.* (p. 24)

The question is then: Can we see it? Or feel it? Do we listen deeply enough to catch these perspectives? The Jungian therapist Thomas Moore (1992) argues that in the modern world, we tend to separate psychology and religion. We believe that emotional problems are linked to family, childhood and trauma, but not to spirituality. He says that our spiritual life needs nourishment, an awareness. When the soul is undermined, we will have various challenges in life, including emotional challenges. Psychology and spirituality must therefore be considered together.

The Italian family therapist Umberta Telfener (2017) describes how working systemically is a way of seeing and acting, an ability to contemplate the whole and appreciate and acknowledge complexity. It is the ability to see both/and, to enhance the connection of opposing elements, to generate a multiverse and allow the context to organize meaning in cultural complexity. She says it is important not to ignore the spiritual domain of humanity.

SEARCHING FOR MEANING

"Man searches for meaning" wrote Viktor Frankl (2004), arguing that meaning is the basic motivation for human life. Human beings are meaning-creating and meaning-seeking; this is a basic humanistic attitude to life. Aron Antonovsky (1987) thought along similar lines with his theory of "sense of coherence". This is a health-promoting perspective, and Antonovsky says that if human life is comprehensive, manageable and meaningful, it will enhance health, coping and well-being. The psychoanalytic psychologist Erich Fromm (2006) also had similar reflections and believed that people need to find answers to their existence. He thinks our basic needs are love, to be part of something bigger, to feel belonging, to find our identity and finally, a need for meaning, orientation and direction in life. Therefore, we need a fundamental trust in life to function as human beings.

To look for meaning in life is to look for patterns and connections, trying to find meaningful aims with our actions and projects in life. To find meaning in life, a person can look for what creates direction through deep life values, in order to live as authentic a life as possible. Through this systemic way of thinking, clients can hopefully gain deeper knowledge of themselves and their relationships. Unreflected judgements can be made more consciously.

We would be the first to admit that getting hold of the spiritual dimension is difficult. It feels much easier to talk about communication and relationships on an interpersonal level. It is so easy to get into patterns and grooves, where the spiritual is not involved. Yes, we hear that people have a belief, that they are spiritual, but how can we use this actively? By excluding clients' spiritual lives, we can lose something important, an important dimension that can help people to achieve greater wholeness, to find inner peace, hope and connection in different crises and difficulties. Hopefully, this book can be of help to reflect further and be a practical guide.

THE BACKGROUND TO THE BOOK

How It All Started

Life has its twists and turns. Sometimes things happen that we do not fully understand—it feels like we are part of something bigger. Sometimes paths cross and something new is created. This was also the case with this book. It is based on a PhD study from 2018 named: *Making Room for Spirituality? Family Therapists' and Clients' Perceptions and Experiences About Spirituality in Family Therapy* (Holmberg 2018). Let us tell you how it all started:

Åse's History
The story of this book goes back to June 2012, when I met Per at a research conference in Oslo. I didn't know him any more than as my former class teacher during my master's degree in systemic family therapy. Per asked me if I was interested in doing a PhD, but my answer was "not yet".

We had no contact during the autumn, but in January 2013 something happened. I was working from home doing some exams. To be honest, it was a bit boring, and then it's easy to get distracted. I went to the website of Per's workplace, VID Specialized University, and there I discovered a job posting. It was a PhD scholarship in family therapy. The first thought that struck me was, "Is this the moment?" The thought was suddenly enticing, and I wondered if I should contact Per again. Should I send him an email? After all, we had spoken in June last year. I decided to give it more time and went out for a walk with my dog. After an hour, I returned and went into Outlook to send an email to Per. And what do you think I found there? Quite surprisingly, an email from Per. I still get goose pimples thinking about this story: it hit me so hard, physically, emotionally and spiritually.

He had written:

> *Dear Åse! Happy New Year! We've got our own PhD programme. "Diaconia, Values and Professional Practice" was approved last year. I read your article in "Focus" (Nordic Family Therapy Journal) and think you should apply for the scholarship we have advertised. Have you seen the advertisement? Do you know about it? Do you want to? Call me for a chat or write. Per*

At that moment I had no doubt, this is the moment. I could not have had a stronger confirmation. It was just as if I understood that this was my mission now. I suddenly felt like part of something bigger, calm but expectant. I wrote back that I was interested and that I would like him to be my supervisor.

It was Per who got me on the track of spirituality. My master's thesis from 2007 dealt with this; there, I interviewed family therapists about the topic. At that time, spirituality was even more under-communicated than today, but I had promised myself (and God) that if I took the new master's degree course, I would delve into that topic, whatever the cost. So, when Per challenged me to delve even deeper, it was as if all the pieces fell into place. It was as if I understood the connection and that now was the time to take this further. The time was now.

THE STUDY DESIGN

This book is based on the PhD: *Making Room for Spirituality? Family Therapists' and Clients' Perceptions and Experiences About Spirituality in Family Therapy* (Holmberg 2018).

The study aimed to explore what spirituality means for family therapy practice, from the perspective of both therapists and clients. A key aim was to find out what kind of meanings the informants associated with the word "spirituality", and what kind of experiences clients and therapists had about including spirituality in therapy. A further aim was to explore how therapists believed their own spirituality influenced their practice.

Constructivist grounded theory (GT) was used as the research and analysis method (Charmaz 2014). There is little research and theory to be found, which meant that constructivist GT could be a useful method. The focus is to learn from practice and let practice be a source for developing a new theory. Kathy Charmaz, the developer of constructivist GT, describes it as "a method of conducting qualitative research that focuses on creating conceptual frameworks or theories through building inductive analysis from the data" (Charmaz 2014, p. 187). The analysis process has a particular focus on meaning, action and process, in an attempt to conceptualize the relationship between experiences and events. The analysis process ends in a "grounded theory", which means an abstract theoretical understanding of the study's experiences. The theory is an interpretation based on the researcher's experience; both the researcher and the informants interpret meaning and action.

Constructivist GT is a modern form of grounded theory. The method retains methodological strategies such as coding, writing memos and "theoretical sampling", but there is a shift in the epistemological foundation. The methodology is influenced by postmodernism, which states that there is no objective reality, and there are as many constructions as there are people. People are influenced by context; reality is socially and culturally created. It is in the interaction between the researcher and informant that data is produced. This is a meaning-making process, and the analysis is a dialogue between the researcher and the data. The developed theory is therefore a social construction.

Twenty-seven informants took part in the study, 15 systemic family therapists and 12 clients, all from Norway. The aim was to have a wide range of informants. The family therapists, 7 women and 8 men, had an average age of 47 years, and had worked for an average of 14.5 years. It was very difficult to find clients as informants. We hoped for help from family therapy centres in the recruitment process, but since spirituality seems to be a topic that is often absent in practice, that was easier said than done. However, Facebook, the study's supervisors and people we knew in the therapy environment were able to help, and we ended up with 8 women and 4 men aged between 40 and 60. All the informants were happy to take part in the study and had a lot on their minds about the topic.

The analysis process ended with 40 codes from the therapists and 55 from the clients. These were developed into five main categories, with many subcategories. The main categories formed the basis for the development of the theory "a map of spiritual and existential literacy", which is further described in Chap. 7.

All the informants were given pseudonyms, which are also used in this book. The names are:

	Systemic therapists	Clients
1.	Edwin	Ewa
2.	Nils	John
3.	Nina	Tone
4.	Siri	Stian
5.	Frode	Anette
6.	Tor	Lisa
7.	Terje	Lisbeth
8.	Magnus	Maja
9.	Tomas	Henrik
10.	Kari	Bjørn
11.	Grete	Ingrid
12.	Ada	Tuva
13.	"The therapy group" Tom, Nora and Lea	

OUR SPIRITUAL LENS

As human beings, we, the authors, are quite different, but there are still some similarities. We are both from Norway. Åse grew up in the mid-60s and Per in the early 50s. Per trained as a psychiatric nurse, while Åse became a clinical social worker and started to use family therapy in the 90s. Per established a master's degree in family therapy at VID Specialized University, where Åse joined as a student in 2000. Per became an inspiration for Åse's family therapeutic work, and for her there was no turning back after learning about this approach. She had taken some courses in family therapy in the mid-90s in Gothenburg in Sweden, and spiritual perspectives had little place there. In one of the main textbooks she read:

> *after all, one cannot find the answers/solutions to the great existential or spiritual questions of life either through psychotherapy, social and mental health or political decisions.* (Lundsbye 2010) (p. 44, our translation)

In the book, we read that it was common for professionals working with people to encounter questions about the meaning of life, where you come from and where you are going, the fear of death, if there is a God or if you can contact him, but these were not suitable perspectives for family therapy work. With such a starting point, it can be difficult to find a way to have a dialogue around these topics, and it can feel easier to close the door if clients dare to say anything about their spiritual reality.

We are both members of the protestant Church of Norway, as are 64% of the Norwegian population. Around 13% of the population are members of a religion or religious community outside the Church of Norway, and only 2.8% are Catholics. We have both had a long spiritual journey, and our systemic lens and our lived life have both influenced us on our journeys. We are naturally quite different people from when we were younger. Nevertheless, we feel humble and still in a learning process, and we realize that there is much more to discover. Of course, we also experience these perspectives differently, and we have had many interesting conversations. We have both experienced the silence in the field around this topic, and Per became an inspiration for Åse to explore it further, professionally speaking.

To sum up, we believe that we all are connected, and that reality is much bigger than we can understand. We have surrendered a dualistic image of God and instead hold that God loves the world and wants contact with us. Life is deeply meaningful, and one's existence has a purpose. Our most important task in the world is to carry on the love of God. The only thing we know is now—and now matters. Human spirituality can make a difference to self, others, nature and life in general.

THE FURTHER STRUCTURE OF THE BOOK

The following chapter (Chap. 2) will examine existing literature on spirituality within our field, including research, professional articles and books, with the hope of inspiring readers to explore this topic further and perhaps even undertake their research projects. Chapter 3 will explore the concept of spirituality in greater depth. We will examine its history and consider various spiritual perspectives, and we have chosen to title this chapter "Spirituality—a Multifaceted Landscape". Chapter 4, entitled "Spirituality in Intercultural Family Therapy", will explore how culture can influence spirituality and religion, and the importance of maintaining cultural sensitivity. Chapter 5 is about obstacles to including spirituality in practice. We will present some obstacles by including reflections from our informants, both therapists and clients. We believe we have a lot to learn from practice. Finally, we will conclude with a critical examination of systemic family therapy.

Part II is titled "Practice and Competence". How can we develop our spirituality and skills for including spirituality in our practice? We start with Chap. 6, "Making Room for Spirituality", which will explore a range of different perspectives linked to a spiritual life. This is an invitation to explore what spiritual life can contain, but also perspectives that can be included in systemic therapy. Chapter 7 brings us to the therapy approach of "Existential psychotherapy", and we explore what we can learn from this. We also include a rather recent health concept, "existential health". This goes deeper than mental health, which is interesting in a systemic context. In Chap. 8, we introduce "A map of spiritual and existential literacy", our theory of practice. We will give an overview of what the concept of literacy can entail and link it to the concept of spirituality. We will also introduce the concept of resonance, which fits in well with spiritual literacy. Chapter 9 is the main chapter and goes into greater detail of our theory of practice concerning spiritual and existential literacy. We include many reflections from our informants in this chapter and find it a useful way to substantiate our theory. It is, after all, a theory of practice! Finally, in Chap. 10, we end with our concluding remarks and tie everything together.

In each chapter you will find some reflection questions. You can answer these alone, or with colleagues or fellow students. The questions will give you the opportunity to go deeper into the topic and reflect on what spirituality means to you, both personally and professionally. We hope that many of you will be inspired, discover the joy and importance of including spirituality in life, and increase your curiosity and openness to clients' spiritual life.

We would recommend buying a nice notebook, where you can write down your reflections—and follow your own spiritual journey.

Reflections

1. What do you think about the topic—so far?
2. Now turn to your feelings: What kind of feelings do you have about this topic? Has anything touched you?
3. In this chapter, Åse told her story leading up to her PhD. If she was your client and told you the story, would you have captured the spiritual dimension? How would you approach the subject, or what questions would you ask to explore her spiritual beliefs and practices?

REFERENCES

Adams, N. (1995). Spirituality, science and therapy. *Australian and New Zealand Journal of Family Therapy, 16*(4), 201–208.

Antonovsky, A. (1987). *Unraveling the mystery of health: how people manage stress and stay well.* Jossey-Bass.

Barker, S., & Scammell, J. (2016). *Psychology for nursing and healthcare professionals: developing compassionate care.* Sage.

Bateson, G. (1979). *Mind and nature: a necessary unity.* Wildwood House.

Bateson, G. (2000). *Steps to an ecology of mind.* University of Chicago Press.

Benner, D. G. (2011). *Soulful spirituality: becoming fully alive and deeply human.* Brazos Press.

Charmaz, K. (2014). *Constructing grounded theory* (2nd ed.). Sage.

Danbolt, L. J. (2014). *Religionspsykologi.* Gyldendal Akademisk.

Drinkwater, K. G., Dagnall, N., Denovan, A., & Williams, C. (2021). Paranormal belief, thinking style and delusion formation: a latent profile analysis of within-individual variations in experience-based paranormal facets. *Frontiers in psychology, 12,* 670959.

Frankl, V. E. (2004). *Man's search for meaning: the classic tribute to hope from the Holocaust.* Rider.

Fromm, E. (2006). *The art of loving* (Fiftieth anniversary ed.). Harper Perennial.

Holm, C. C., Karlsson, B. E., & Holmberg, Å. (2023). Experiences of spirituality of in- and out-patients in mental health facilities: A thematic synthesis of qualitative studies. *Journal of spirituality in mental health, ahead-of-print*(ahead-of-print), 1–30. https://doi.org/10.1080/19349637.2023.2213455

Holmberg, Å. (2018). *Making room for spirituality?: family therapists' and clients' perceptions and experiences about spirituality in family therapy* VID Specialized University]. Oslo.

Holmberg, Å., & Jensen, P. (2024). Spirituality: A meaningful philosophy of life and a "lifeline" in times of crises. In (1 ed., Vol. 1, pp. 122–132). Routledge. https://doi.org/10.4324/9781003308096-13

Holmberg, Å., Jensen, P., & Vetere, A. (2021). Spirituality–a forgotten dimension? Developing spiritual literacy in family therapy practice. *Journal of Family Therapy, 43*(1), 78–95.

Holmberg, Å., & Karlsson, B. (2023). Giving Resonance and Room to Spirituality in Systemic Practice. In (pp. 81–96). Cham: Springer International Publishing. https://doi.org/10.1007/978-3-031-30526-9_6

Janis, S. (2008). *Spirituality for dummies.* Wiley Publishing Inc.

Larner, G. (2017). Spiritual Dialogues in Family Therapy. *Australian and New Zealand Journal of Family Therapy, 38*(1), 125–141. https://doi.org/10.1002/anzf.1207

Lundsbye, M. (2010). *Familjeterapins grunder: ett interaktionistiskt perspektiv, baserat på system-, process- och kommunikationsteori*. Natur och Kultur.

McGilchrist, I. (2021). *The matter with things: our brains, our delusions and the unmaking of the world*. Perspectiva Press.

Moore, T. (1992). *Care of the soul: a guide for cultivating depth and sacredness in everyday life*. HarperCollins.

Rohr, R. (2021). *Breathing under Water: Spirituality and the Twelve Steps*. Franciscan Media.

Stripp, T. A., Wehberg, S., Büssing, A., Koenig, H. G., Balboni, T. A., VanderWeele, T. J., Søndergaard, J., & Hvidt, N. C. (2023). Spiritual needs in Denmark: a population-based cross-sectional survey linked to Danish national registers. *The Lancet Regional Health–Europe, 28*.

Telfener, U. (2017). Becoming through Belonging: The Spiritual Dimension in Psychotherapy. *Australian and New Zealand Journal of Family Therapy, 38*(1), 156–167. https://doi.org/10.1002/anzf.1199

Walsh, F. (1999). *Spiritual resources in family therapy*. Guilford Press.

Walsh, F. (2009b). *Spiritual resources in family therapy*. Guilford Press.

Aadnanes, P. M. (2012). *Livssyn* (4. utg. ed.). Universitetsforl.

CHAPTER 2

Experiences from the Field

The art of hearing heartbeats.
—Jan-Philipp Sendker

We will now go back in history and consider the voices who have tried to incorporate spirituality into family therapy practice. There are some, although they never had a huge impact. History can help us to understand the present. Perhaps some ideas from the past can enrich us today.

The family therapy movement started in the 1950s in both the USA and Europe and was based on some 100-year-old psychotherapy traditions. Family therapy developed from different sources and in different institutions and countries. Today family therapy is often called systemic psychotherapy, and systemic thinking and communication theory can be seen as the framework for clinical practice.

First, we will provide some historical background of spirituality and psychotherapy. We will then mention some family therapists who have contributed to the spiritual perspective and explore some articles that have been published on the subject in the last three decades. Finally, we will present some of the research in this area from the last decade.

Å. Holmberg, P. Jensen, *Working with Spirituality in Family Systemic Practice*, Palgrave Texts in Counselling and Psychotherapy, https://doi.org/10.1007/978-3-031-77310-5_2

HISTORY OF SPIRITUALITY AND PSYCHOTHERAPY

In terms of human history, the psychotherapy movement is very recent. Before there was anything called psychotherapy, for millennia, witch doctors, shamans and spiritual leaders provided psychological, emotional and spiritual healing (Patterson et al. 2000). In many cultures, mental health and family problems are still treated by spiritual leaders. We also see this in our own culture, among the Sami in the north, and in more closed religious communities. The medical discourse has dominated Western society and here we probably have something to learn from the East. Eastern culture and medicine have to a greater extent integrated a holistic view of human beings, involving body, mind and spirit (Walsh 2009b). Spirituality in Eastern philosophy aims at balance and harmony and seems to be infused into everyday life to a greater degree.

Initially, the relationship between spirituality and psychotherapy became problematic. Sigmund Freud, the father of psychoanalysis, was very critical of religion, and called it "a universal neurosis". Religion was also called mystical experiences, ego regression, neurotic symbolic externalizing and mass psychosis and was an expression of the ideology of the dominant class (Lukoff et al. 1992; Lundsbye 2010).

However, some psychotherapists worked more holistically, such as Carl Jung, William James and Viktor Frankl, but the positivist paradigm and the medical model emerged as the dominant epistemology in the field. This resulted in higher status and scientific credibility for evidence-based practice and measurable objective observations (Walsh 2009a).

The history of mental health in the West shows that it was very important to keep spiritual issues out of psychotherapy. Therapists were trained not to include spiritual or religious life in treatment. That part of the human being was separated off and could in some cases be referred to a priest or pastoral care. This in turn made many church leaders warn against psychotherapy and instead encouraged people to seek help within the congregation (Walsh 2009b). Our experience is that this still happens today, mostly in conservative Christian communities or Muslim contexts.

Lutheran teaching has influenced much of society, creating an ontological distinction between the divine and the eternal. The Bible text "Pay back, therefore, Caesar's things to Caesar, but God's things to God" (Matt. 22:21) has been interpreted as a dualism, a distinction between the kingdom of the world and the kingdom of God. This has probably helped to maintain the distinction between religious and secular practice, between secular psychotherapy and pastoral care. "Natural knowledge" has become part of science, while "supernatural knowledge" is part of religion.

In our part of the world, the split between the worldly and the spiritual has continued to increase. Science focuses on the rational and biological side of humans, and religious institutions on the spiritual. Because of the positivist influence, science became distinguished from theology and philosophy. In the field of psychology, spirituality was often expressed in over-simplified and stereotypical terms (Pargament 2007). Consequently, mental health professionals tend to either ignore or pathologize the spiritual or religious part of life (Swinton 2001). Surprisingly, these ideas still exist in mental health and psychiatry, over a hundred years after the entry of the psychotherapy movement. We have not come any further!

A related aspect is the myth of neutrality, which existed for many decades, and still does. Therapists were trained to be objective and unbiased and not reveal their spiritual practice and values (Walsh 2009b). We have called it a myth because we believe it is impossible to be neutral. As therapists, we always will influence the therapy process. We are part of the therapy system. Both our analogue and digital language will "reveal ourselves", what we punctuate, and which questions we ask—and don't ask. Based on our research, but also our own experiences, we think it will be felt whether therapists are open to the spiritual or not.

SPIRITUALITY VOICES AMONG FAMILY THERAPISTS

In this section, we will start with a woman from the early days of the family therapy movement, namely Virginia Satir. She was a social worker but later became a family therapist. Her model was called "humanistic family therapy", and she had an intrapsychic and interpersonal focus. The relationship with the therapist was very important (Satir 1991). In the change process, she was interested in the connection to the self, which she called human spiritual essence. The inner self of a person could be described with different words: spirit, soul, life force, essence, core and being. During her work, she encouraged her clients to access their positive spiritual energy for healing, to live in balance with their life force. For her, spirituality was to be open to and in contact with a power with multiple names, which could also be God. Interestingly, Satir's model never achieved a breakthrough in the West, but her ideas have been a major factor in the therapeutic movement in the East (Banmen and Maki-Banmen 2014).

Let us also mention Jim Lantz, who in the 1970s developed a model called "existential family therapy". It was based on ideas from existential philosophy and existential literature (Lantz 1994a, 1994b). He wrote several articles over 25 years and was influenced by the founder of "logotherapy", Viktor Frankl and also the French philosopher Gabriel Marcel.

In this approach, the clients' reflections about meaning-making were in focus, and the key was to turn this perspective into action. Lantz criticized the family therapy movement of the time, which he felt was too problem-focused with paradoxical interventions. He preferred a more "mystery-centred approach" where the important points were inter-subjectivity, empathy, human freedom, relationship, commitment and mutual participatory experience. Love was referred to as a basic healing process, where spirituality was the centre of human lives.

Another figure, still working and active in the field, is Harry Aponte. He has gone so far as to say that spirituality is the heart of therapy (Aponte 2002). Although he is aware that there can be many challenges linked to spiritual and religious issues, such as culture, tradition and religious institutions, he believes spirituality is to be found hidden in all people's hearts and is manifested under many names and guises (Aponte 2009).

Froma Walsh is also an important contributor of spirituality to the family therapy field. She is the editor of *Spiritual resources in family therapy* (Walsh 2009b) and has written several articles about the topic. She is interested in spirituality for coping, healing and resilience and says that clients who sense that spirituality does not belong to therapy do not include it. Walsh says that spirituality involves streams of experience that flow through all aspects of life and argues that a systemic approach to practice needs to encompass a holistic biopsychosocial-spiritual orientation. The spiritual beliefs of people will infiltrate different aspects of life, such as dealing with adversity, their approach to health, their experience of suffering and their preferred pathway in recovery (Walsh 2012a). Walsh and her colleagues have provided valuable contributions as to how spirituality can be included in family therapy practice, such as how to relate to different cultural aspects of religion. She also includes topics such as morality, forgiveness, death and the use of rituals (Walsh 2009a).

Current Books

There are few books on the market about family therapy and spirituality. In addition to those already mentioned, Erickson and Carlson (2014) have written "Spirituality and Family Therapy". This book includes guidelines for therapists who are unsure about how to integrate spiritual issues into their practice, spiced with detailed case studies that reveal how and why faith is a vital part of many clients' lives.

We would also like to mention a book from the Tao Institute in the US: *Spirituality, Social Construction and Relational Processes: Essays and Reflections* (Bidwell 2016). Here we find a wide range of authors who share their experiences of a spiritual and religious life, and how these perspectives are integrated into their practice. One of the contributors, Kenneth Gergen, has published several articles on the topic (Gergen 1999). He believes that the divine is a process within which we exist and from which we cannot remove ourselves and states that the sacred is "immanent in all human affairs" (2009b).

In 2018, David Trimble edited the book*: Engaging with Spirituality in Family Therapy: Meeting in Sacred Space* (2018), in the book series AFTA SpringerBriefs in Family Therapy. In an advertisement for the book, we can read:

> *Chapter authors build on their own narratives of spiritual journey as they inform conversation with clients whose faith perspectives include Christianity, Judaism, Islam, African and Native American spiritual practice, Taoism, and Sikhism. These powerful dialogues illuminate the deeper tasks of therapy and offer significant opportunities for all family members to be involved in creating meaning and healing together.*

In the same book series is *Socially Just Religious and Spiritual Interventions: Ethical Uses of Therapeutic Power*, edited by Elisabeth Esmiol Wilson and Lindsey Nice (2018). This work answers essential questions in family therapy by exploring the ethical use of religion and spirituality in the clinical context. Its justice-informed framework explores how to employ the spiritual as a source of resilience and empowerment as well as counter harmful spiritual and religious influences in situations that cause families and couples stress, particularly relating to gender, sexuality, race, culture and identity.

A recent book related to systemic supervision and training is titled *Spirituality in Systemic Family Therapy Supervision and Training* (Coyle 2022a). Suzanne Coyle, who is from the US, addresses systemic supervision and training and explores a systemic approach to the development of the self.

Finally, let us mention a book from our environment at VID Specialized University in Oslo, *New Horizons in Systemic Practice with Adults* (Grover et al. 2023). This is a practical book which explores new applications of systemic understanding in practice. There are spiritual perspectives in several chapters in the book, and Åse has collaborated with Bengt Karlsson on a chapter called *Giving Resonance and Room to Spirituality in Systemic Practice* (Holmberg and Carlsson 2023). This chapter explores the concept of spirituality in different ways, underpinned by voices from a study of unemployed young adults in Norway.

Theoretical Articles from the Last Three Decades

Although spirituality has not been particularly prominent in the field of family therapy, several therapists have tried to highlight the topic by writing different types of articles. We will mention some of them here.

Culture and Spirituality

In the early 1980s, culture and race were raised as an important topic in family therapy. Several authors called for families to be viewed from a cultural perspective, where sociocultural and spiritual factors were included. Examples of cultural aspects are morality, forgiveness, death and the use of rituals.

Therapists have written that systemic thinking has to be valid for all families regardless of cultural differences. Some also criticized the field by stating that when culture was discussed in practice and training, spiritual and religious perspectives were left out (Falicov 1995; Martinez 1994).

Walsh (2003) joined the debate, stating that it was important to broaden clinical perspectives to the increasing diversity and complexity in society. Today we have many interfaith couples or multifaith families, and cultural influences are interwoven in many aspects of life. It is therefore important to approach spiritual diversity in clinical practice and ask about beliefs and practices, but also spiritual resources and spiritual sources of distress.

Telfener (2017) has also highlighted the aspect of culture, pointing out that we all have bio, cultural, spiritual and psychological needs. These elements are shared, tacitly, in constructions of meaning. She believes that all intersubjective discourses are by definition cultural and should be made explicit in our common therapeutic work.

Another project that connects spirituality and culture is "Social GRRAAACCEESS" from the UK (Fig. 2.1). The UK Association for Family Therapy and Systemic Practice has initiated a project in which systemic therapists work in an inclusive and non-discriminatory way and develop self-reflexivity in relation to what they call "Social GGRRAAACCEEESSS", which means the social identities of *gender, geography, race, religion, age, ability, appearance, class, culture, ethnicity, education, employment, sexuality, sexual orientation* and *spirituality*. Several articles have been written on this topic (Burnham 2005, 2012; Pearson 2017).

Pearson (2017) says that working with clients' spiritual and religious experiences requires paying close attention to self-reflexivity, and that

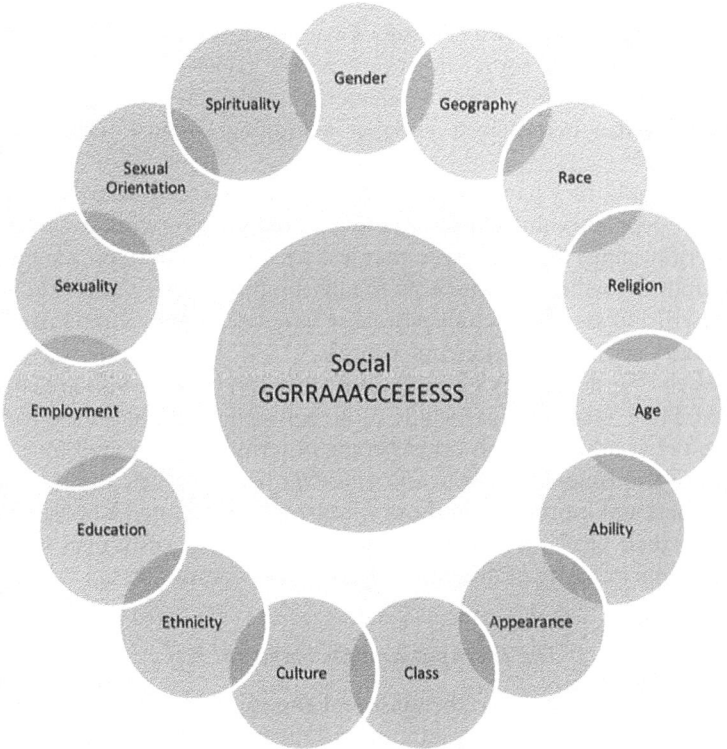

Fig. 2.1 Social graces

there is a need for competence, training and supervision for therapists concerning these issues. She believes that family therapists, in dealing with religion and spirituality, have the potential to enable, limit or prevent clients from addressing problems or accessing resources. Pearson argues that systemic practitioners share a commitment to facilitate healing by utilizing clients' meanings and social networks and by establishing a relationship based on acknowledgement as well as differences.

In New Zealand "Just Therapy Team" has actively promoted spirituality connected to culture in their practice. They have worked closely with the indigenous population and their focus areas are culture, gender and socioeconomic disadvantage. Interestingly, they say they have moved away from medical terminology such as diagnosis, causes and cures and have developed a language which articulates the key values in their work. These principles are belonging, sacredness and liberation (Campbell et al. 2001).

According to the "Just Therapy Group", it is crucial to understand issues of belonging, roots and where people come from. They say it is important to look for liberating elements in their shared history and to ground human beings in a sense of belonging to their history, place and people.

In addition, they have developed a concept of sacredness, which means they see people's vulnerable stories as a sacred gift. To work together on issues of healing, they have seen that it is necessary to develop a language of sacredness, which includes ways to talk about spirituality. Soul and body are fused, and sacredness and spirituality have been their central image for exchanges within the therapeutic process.

For the "Just Therapy Group" spirituality and relationships are closely linked. Here, relationships include those between people and the environment, between people and other people in terms of justice and love, and finally relationships between people and their heritage, their ancestry, their forefathers and mothers, and those who have gone before. A holistic view inspires their views of humanity and the sacredness of human life and respects the integrity of different cultures (Waldegrave 2003).

The Therapist and the Spiritual Self

Another perspective is the therapist and the spiritual self. Harris (1998) encouraged therapists to pay attention to their spiritual self because it will make them more open to the spiritual dimension in different families. Harris developed a training programme for family therapists which focused on spiritual growth. The aim was to help students to understand the spiritual nature of human beings. Lum (2002) follows up on this and says the use of the self of the therapist enables the therapeutic process to be strength-oriented, creative and respectful. Following Satir, Lum says that it is important for therapists to accept feelings as they are and to try to live in harmony with others, the world and finally with oneself. All human beings have a life force that has an aspect of divinity and spirituality. As therapists we need to turn the question to our own life: "What do I know about the sense of the divine in my own life?" Therapists need contact with their soul to be able to process the client's spiritual exploration.

Religiosity and God

It is interesting to note that much of the early literature on spirituality comes from the US. There, religious aspects are incorporated into culture differently, and there seems to be greater collaboration between pastoral clinical services and family therapy. Articles from the 1980s, 1990s and early 2000s seem more connected to a Christian tradition or interdisciplinary, including both clinical and religious realms (Blanton 2005; Hoogestraat and Trammel 2003; Wendel 2003). Butler and Harper (1994) introduced a concept called "the divine triangle", partly based on the approach of the family therapist Murray Bowen (Bowen 1978). Here, God was presented in a couple-God triangle, thus a triangulation process. This was presented as a powerful tool for religious couples. God was also presented as a stabilizing interpersonal part of families' daily transactions and part of the change process. Griffith and Rotter (1999) went so far as to say that overlooking clients' religious (and spiritual) lives is working in a vacuum and may be an unethical practice. Therapists should relate to "sacred" topics with respect and gentleness. It might help to rework families' spiritual orientation.

Spirituality in Clinical Training

As mentioned, spirituality has mostly been absent in family therapy education and clinical training, and several voices have highlighted the need for a change. Haug (1998b) feels that family therapist training has focused on epistemologies, models and intervention techniques, rather than training in appropriate awareness and use of the self. This includes the therapist's meaning system and beliefs. The introduction of social construction has increased the focus on the self of the therapists, but the spirituality dimension has still been excluded.

Neden et al. (2011) attempted to emphasize spirituality dialogues in family therapy education. They developed a model with the aim of highlighting connections to spiritual resources in teaching and supervision. Initially, students and teachers discussed a possible arrangement in line with the Association for Family Therapy and Systemic Practice in the UK. Both teachers and students tried to answer the following questions:

1. What has been your spiritual journey?
2. How influential is your spirituality in determining your ideas about:

   (a) family relationships?
   (b) therapy?
   (c) training?
   (d) mental health?

3. Do you ask families or supervisors about their experience of religion and spirituality?
4. What constrains you from introducing this into conversations?
5. How do your spiritual beliefs influence/enable/constrain your conversations?
6. How do you position yourself in relation to spiritual belief systems that condone or promote oppressive practices?
7. In what way do you (or do you not) relate spirituality to your experience of organized religion?
8. What meaning are we making about the differences and similarities between our stories?
9. What are we learning through these differences?

The individual answers were then reflected upon by others in a desire to expand mutual understanding. This in turn led to new questions they could share.

Spirituality and Social Construction

In the 1980s, the family therapy movement was influenced by social constructivism. This philosophical trend set the tone in psychology and social science, with its acknowledgement that reality, knowledge and meaning are created in linguistic construction between people. Narrative practice was developed in the wave of social constructivism, and Carlson and Erickson (2000) wrote an article highlighting narrative therapy as an opening to include spiritual and religious aspects in life, through a focus on clients' values. They believed that the concept of multivoices or multiverse from Maturana (1992) had opened up a space for marginalized voices to achieve legitimacy in the field. This was an acknowledgement of the complexity of systems, and through this, alternative paths of knowledge and experience could become more viable.

This was also supported by Thayne (1998), who said that humans were classified by society and mental health, and their religiosity was pathologized. Therapists should allow clients to construct their spirituality and have a teachable attitude. Spirituality is complex, not one-directional. Thayne encouraged therapists to be co-authors with their clients, where new meanings could evolve through language. However, clients have to be the first author of their own spiritual story, and Thayne said that this joint work can help therapists to understand the vulnerability of sharing spiritual or religious life. Thayne also considered it important to see the potential for health in the spiritual stories of the clients and felt that therapists must confront their stereotypes and prejudgements and become self-aware of their own biases. An environment of togetherness will make the client feel safer, and it will be easier to recognize the emotional level connected to the client's values. This is not a technique in a modernist sense, but a "not-knowing position" which helps therapists to be curious and discuss the meaning that is most significant for each client.

Tools for Including Spirituality in Family Therapy

How can we include spirituality in systemic family therapy in practice? Froma Walsh (2009b) says:

> Until recently, spirituality was regarded as 'off limits' in clinical training and practice, leaving most therapists and counsellors uncertain how to approach it, if at all. (p. xi)

It seems that there is room for new creative angles and a lot to explore. However, as you will see in the recommended books or articles, there are various ideas about how to incorporate spiritual and/or religious perspectives into practice. Another author is Hodge (2005), who has introduced five different spiritual assessment approaches:

1. **Verbal spiritual histories**—different questions which explore experiences from childhood and family life and how these affect life today.

2. **A spiritual life map**—a pictorial delineation of a client's spiritual journey. Like roadmaps, spiritual life maps tell us where we have come from, where we are now, and where we are going.
3. **Spiritual genogram**—These approaches illustrate the flow of spiritual patterns across at least three generations in a manner analogous to traditional genograms. This can help therapists and clients to understand the flow of historically rooted patterns through time.
4. **Spiritual ecomap**—This focuses on the client's current, existential/spiritual relationship. These stories highlight clients' present existential relationships to spiritual assets. The heart of the spiritual ecomap is the relationships between the family system and the spiritual systems.
5. **Spiritual ecogram**—This is a combination of genogram and ecomap. Ecograms tap information that exists in space and across time and depict the connections between past history and present functioning.

RESEARCH ON SYSTEMIC FAMILY THERAPY AND SPIRITUALITY

There is little research on spirituality to be found in our field. Many professional articles have been published in recent years, but the research is still in its infancy. We will refer to some studies from 2010 onwards. Our own study is the only one we have found that includes a client perspective (Holmberg 2018).

First, we will present studies which explore the concept of spirituality. Miller and Sheppard (Miller McInnes and Van Ness Sheppard 2014) conducted a qualitative study in which 141 family therapy graduate students participated. A Foucauldian analysis was used, and four discourses of themes embodied the majority of responses:

1. Spirituality as a relational connection	A relationship with self, connection with other people, personal atonement with the divine, connection with nature.
2. Spirituality as individually defined	Spirituality was constructed in a personal and individualistic manner, a clear "I-position"
3. Spirituality as relative and unspecific	Reflected a relativistic worldview
4. Spirituality as a manifestation of power dynamics	A power dynamics on different levels, a powerful driving force in life

The study shows that spirituality can be difficult to capture in words, especially when therapists find that the subject is not recognized in their profession. However, there is a will to meet the spirituality of the client with respect and acknowledgement.

We will now turn to a qualitative study from Norway with 12 therapists, including family therapists (Ulland and DeMarinis 2014). Semi-structured interviews were analysed using systematic text condensation. Instead of using the word spirituality, existential information was used.

The study aimed to explore how therapists in a mental health context understand and handle existential information. The therapists used words like existential orientation, meaning-making, worldview, spirituality and religiosity. The authors argued that the philosophy of mental health seems to be based on therapists' existential orientation and their professional sociocultural context. Working on one's own spiritual cultural story seems to be of great importance for the therapist's ability to include these issues in practice. The informants reported that existential issues were missing in their education, which has led to them not knowing how to integrate spirituality into therapy. However, the therapists wanted to become more skilled in how to include spirituality in practice, and also called for acceptance and support from their leaders to include the topic.

There is also a quantitative study from the US by Carlson et al. (2011), where they explored family therapists' and family therapy educators' personal and professional experiences of spirituality. Both groups indicated that spirituality was important in their life, but still reported some level of uncertainty about how to include spirituality in practice. However, the students wanted to learn more about the subject and said that working on their own spirituality was necessary to help clients with their spiritual life. Interestingly, the students had several ideas about how to include clients' spirituality in relation to coping skills:

1. Using spiritual language or concepts
2. Discussion of spiritual symbols
3. Praying privately for clients
4. Discussing the meaning of life and death
5. Using spiritual issues to connect clients to others in a community context

The students felt constrained when discussing spirituality in their professional community, and they had received no training. There was also a need for supervision and discussions about how to deal with the differences between spirituality and religion.

Two more quantitative studies from the family therapy student environment should be included. The first one is by McNeil et al. (2012). Among the 135 students in the study, the majority reported that spirituality and religion were not included in their education, and about half wanted to learn more about how to include these topics in practice. The researchers saw that if the topic was important privately to students, it was easier for them to incorporate spiritual aspects into practice. The more important the topic was to the students, the keener they were to include the topic in therapy and training.

The second study is by Carlson et al. (2014), who developed an online survey using the "Spirituality in Clinical Training Scale". Respondents were 341 master's and doctoral students. Besides testing the validity of the measuring instrument, the study aimed to measure the importance of spirituality to the students, their spiritual clinical competence and their spiritual beliefs. The results revealed that increased clinical competence led to an awareness of one's own values, but also the client's values, which made students aware of not imposing their own values on clients. The findings also showed that if spirituality is an important dimension in students' lives, it will also be more important to them in their practice. The more the students reflected on their spiritual life, the more comfortable they became to reflect on this with clients.

We will end this section with two qualitative studies, the first from Balmer et al. (2012), a phenomenological study with eight so-called secular-based family therapists in the US. The findings showed that the therapists lacked training, but still tried to incorporate clients' spirituality appropriately. The therapists tried to relate to clients with curiosity, but were sometimes anxious and did not know how to handle the information in a meaningful way. However, they realized the importance of focusing on the client's spiritual and therapeutic needs, not their own.

A more recent study is by Nadir Khan (2022). He is a family systemic psychotherapist and a member of WCEN Muslim Leadership Network which offers systemic training and therapy to faith communities in south London and is also a member of the Muslim Counsellor and Psychotherapist Network. He has conducted a qualitative study of systemic training and practice for Muslim community leaders as part of an innovative project in London.

In an interpretive phenomenological analysis study, he interviewed three Muslim leaders who had completed two years of systemic training as part of an innovative project in an inner-city area. The findings showed that the participants acknowledged that most systemic principles and interventions were complementary to religious constructs and could be applied in their community work. Being part of a Muslim cohort, the skilful management of cultural sensitivity by the instructors, and opportunities for faith-based perspectives to be appreciated and engaged with as part of the meaning-making process were all key aspects of a positive learning experience. We feel that this study is an important contribution to building bridges and dialogue in today's society.

Another study from the UK by Lewis J. Blair (2015) has explored how psychotherapists' spirituality affected their practice. The therapists suggested that their spirituality enriched their work and had an integrating synthesizing function in their identity. They felt that it was important to reflect on self-knowledge and practise self-reflection on how the therapist's spirituality influenced practice. They believed that without reflection, therapists would have a huge blind spot, making it unpleasant to meet clients. Responding to the client's spirituality had to be one of the therapist's skills, which also involved an awareness of one's own spiritual life.

An important focus was learning from the client. However, the therapists found it more difficult when clients were more dogmatic or fundamentalist, when they were perceived as more rigid and when their views did not resonate with the therapist's spiritual framework. The therapists experienced a spiritual silence in education and practice, which meant that they had to find their own way. This is also supported by a qualitative study from the US, where therapists felt isolated concerning spirituality, which made them confused, uncertain and in a dilemma as to how they should approach the topic with clients (Magaldi-Dopman et al. 2011). Lack of training and focus on this often led to distance from the clients and a lack of self-awareness. There was a big risk that the topic could be overlooked when their philosophy of life did not match that of the client.

LEARNING FROM THE HISTORY

The field of family therapy is constantly evolving, and it is interesting to see what we can learn from neighbouring fields, and our history. We mentioned initially Carl Jung, who was concerned with the unconscious, like Freud, but he had a much broader understanding of what controls us. Jung was concerned with the metaphysical, was resource-oriented and promoted the creative and the healing in the psyche. He was concerned that we should listen to our dreams, write them down and try to interpret them as far as possible in the language of consciousness. He was concerned with distinguishing between the ego and the self and believed that the self was the real driving force in every human being. A power that is an image of the eternal man, where we can feel a unity with the cosmos. By listening inwardly, we will gain increasingly better contact with the self. This part of man is actively creative, our spirituality. Jung believed at the same time that we must be willing to let go of selfish desires and needs, and not be controlled by unconscious forces. He emphasized the need for dialogue both with society and the subconscious (Jung 1966; Nordhelle and Sakhi 2019). When clients have deeper problems such as anxiety and depression, it can be important to explore what clients believe the "roots" may be, and what may be protective, on a physical, psychological, social and spiritual level.

Viktor Frankel and his logotherapy, developed after several years in a concentration camp during the Second World War, concluded that the human will for meaning was the most important driving force of human beings (Frankl 1992). This is therefore about a deeper meaning in life, linked to our values and attitudes. The question is how concerned we family therapists are with the deeper meaning of life in clients' lives—and whether we use this actively to promote hope, faith and movement in difficult life situations.

These are just a couple of examples of older sources that can enrich us with the challenges we face today. In our society today, we have, among other things, many psychological challenges that affect single individuals, couples or family life, families and society at large. We don't think it's enough to explore what this does between people, but think, in addition, we need to delve deeper into people's inner lives.

Existential Struggles

Emmy and Peter came to couples therapy. Emmy was distraught, Peter was her great love. Peter, on the other hand, was unsure of his feelings for Emmy, unsure if he wanted to continue. We explored many perspectives in their lives, but Peter believed that it wasn't really about Emmy. He was filled with his own uneasiness, and finally concluded that he believed this was existential. What was the real meaning of life? What would he use his life for? His grandparents had recently died, people he had a very close relationship with. He was an only child, had no contact with his father and he suddenly felt very lonely. He longed for community, belonging, being part of something bigger. Emmy, who was very tired of waiting for Peter's feelings, thought that Peter needed help with these thoughts and feelings.

SUMMARY

We now have been on a brief journey during a part of the history of psychotherapy and how the spiritual perspective has been incorporated and developed in the field of family therapy. It has been quiet, with only a few voices. But something has changed in the last decade. Nowadays we are experiencing a new openness and interest in the topic. We notice it among students, therapists and the staff in education and supervision. Students have asked for more teaching on the subject. When it comes to research, there is a great need for more in the systemic family therapy field. And maybe you, who are reading this right now, have an emerging idea?

Reflections

1. What do you think we can learn from the historical perspectives in this regard?
2. How can these ideas better be incorporated into your practice or supervision?
3. What kind of spiritual perspectives do you think should be further explored in research?
4. What kind of research would you like to do?

REFERENCES

Aponte, H. J. (2002). Spirituality: The heart of therapy. In T. D. Carlson, Erickson, M.J. (Ed.), *Spirituality and Family Therapy*. Routledge.

Aponte, H. J. (2009). The stress of povertry and the comfort of spirituality. In F. Walsh (Ed.), *Spiritual resourses in family therapy* (2 ed., pp. 125–140). The Guliford Press.

Balmer, T. D., Van Asselt, K. W., Walker, C., & Kennedy, B. R. (2012). A Phenomenological Study of Spiritual Values in Secular-Based Marriage and Family Therapists [Article]. *Journal of spirituality in mental health, 14*(4), 242–258. https://doi.org/10.1080/19349637.2012.730466

Banmen, J., & Maki-Banmen, K. (2014). What Has Become of Virginia Satir's Therapy Model Since She Left Us in 1988? *Journal of Family Psychotherapy, 25*(2), 117–131.

Bidwell, D. E. (2016). *Spirituality, Social Construction and Relational Processes: Essays and Reflections*. A Tao Institute Publication.

Blair, L. J. (2015). The influence of therapists' spirituality on their practice: A grounded theory exploration. *Counselling and Psychotherapy Research, 15*(3), 161–170.

Blanton, P. G. (2005). Narrative Family Therapy and Spiritual Direction: Do They Fit? [Article]. *Journal of Psychology & Christianity*, *24*(1), 68–79. http://search.ebscohost.com/login.aspx?direct=true&db=afh&AN=16802929&site=ehost-live

Bowen, M. (1978). *Family therapy in clinical practice*. Aronson.

Burnham, J. (2005). Relational reflexivity: a tool for socially constructing therapeutic relationships. *The space between: Experience, context and process in the therapeutic relationship*. London: Karnac.

Burnham, J. (2012). Developments in Social GRRRAAACCEEESSS: visible–invisible and voiced–unvoiced. *Culture and Reflexivity in Systemic Psychotherapy. Mutual Perspectives*, 139–160.

Butler, M. H., & Harper, J. M. (1994). The divine triangle: God in the marital system of religious couples. *Family Process*, *33*(3), 277–286.

Campbell, W., Tamasese, K., & Waldegrave, C. (2001). Just Therapy. In D. Denborough (Ed.), *Family Therapy: Exploring the filed`s past, present & possible futures*. Dulwich Centre Publications.

Carlson, T., & Erickson, M. J. (2000). Re-authoring spiritual narratives: God in persons' relational identity stories. *Journal of Systemic Therapies*, *19*(2), 65–83.

Carlson, T., McGeorge, C., & Anderson, A. (2011). The Importance of Spirituality in Couple and Family Therapy: A Comparative Study of Therapists' and Educators' Beliefs [Article]. *Contemporary Family Therapy: An International Journal*, *33*(1), 3–16. https://doi.org/10.1007/s10591-010-9136-0

Carlson, T., McGeorge, C., & Toomey, R. (2014). Establishing the Validity of the Spirituality in Clinical Training Scale: Measuring the Level of Integration of Spirituality and Religion in Family Therapy Training [Article]. *Contemporary Family Therapy: An International Journal*, *36*(2), 310–325. https://doi.org/10.1007/s10591-013-9278-y

Coyle, S. M. (2022a). Spirituality in Individual, Tandem, and Group Supervision. In *Spirituality in Systemic Family Therapy Supervision and Training* (pp. 73–93). Springer.

Erickson, M. J., & Carlson, T. (2014). *Spirituality and family therapy*. Routledge.

Esmiol Wilson, E., & Nice, L. (2018). *Socially Just Religious and Spiritual Interventions: Ethical Uses of Therapeutic Power* (1st 2018. ed.). Cham: Springer International Publishing AG. https://doi.org/10.1007/978-3-030-01986-0

Falicov, C. J. (1995). Training to think culturally: A multidimensional comparative framework. *Family process*, *34*(4), 373–388.

Frankl, V. E. (1992). *Man's search for meaning: an introduction to logotherapy* (4th ed.). Beacon Press.

Gergen, K. J. (1999). *An invitation to social construction*. Sage.

Gergen, K. J. (2009b). *Relational being: beyond self and community*. Oxford University Press.

Griffith, B. A., & Rotter, J. C. (1999). Families and spirituality: Therapists as facilitators. *The Family Journal, 7*(2), 161–164.

Grover, T., Myra, S. M., & Axberg, U. (2023). *New Horizons in Systemic Practice with Adults* (1 ed.). Cham: Springer International Publishing AG. https://doi.org/10.1007/978-3-031-30526-9

Harris, S. M. (1998). Finding a forest among trees: Spirituality hiding in family therapy theories. *Journal of Family Studies, 4*(1), 77–86.

Haug, I. (1998b). Spirituality as a Dimension of Family Therapists' Clinical Training. *Contemporary family therapy, 20*(4), 471–483. https://doi.org/1 0.1023/A:1021628132514

Hodge, D. R. (2005). Spiritual assessment in marital and family therapy: A methodological framework for selecting from among six qualitative assessment tools. *Journal of marital and Family Therapy, 31*(4), 341–356.

Holmberg, Å. (2018). *Making room for spirituality?: family therapists' and clients' perceptions and experiences about spirituality in family therapy* VID Specialized University]. Oslo.

Holmberg, Å., & Carlsson, B. (2023). Givin resonans and room to spirituality in systemic practice. In T. Grøver, S. M. Myra, & U. Axberg (Eds.), *New Horizons in Systemic Practice with Adults* (pp. 81–96). Palgrave Macmillan.

Hoogestraat, T., & Trammel, J. (2003). Spiritual and Religious Discussions in Family Therapy: Activities to Promote Dialogue [Article]. *American Journal of Family Therapy, 31*(5), 413. https://doi.org/10.1080/01926180390224049

Jung, C. G. (1966). *Psychology and religion*. Yale University Press.

Khan, N. (2022). A qualitative exploration of systemic training and practice for Muslim community leaders as part of an innovative project in an inner-city area. *Journal of Family Therapy, 44*(1), 124–141.

Lantz, J. (1994a). Mystery in family therapy. *Contemporary family therapy, 16*(1), 53–66.

Lantz, J. (1994b). Primary and secondary reflection in existential family therapy. *Contemporary family therapy, 16*(4), 315–327.

Lukoff, D., Turner, R., & Lu, F. (1992). Transpersonal psychology research review: Psychoreligious dimensions of healing. *The Journal of Transpersonal Psychology, 24*(1), 41.

Lum, W. (2002). The use of self of the therapist. *Contemporary family therapy, 24*(1), 181–197.

Lundsbye, M. (2010). *Familjeterapins grunder: ett interaktionistiskt perspektiv, baserat på system-, process- och kommunikationsteori*. Natur och Kultur.

Magaldi-Dopman, D., Park-Taylor, J., & Ponterotto, J. G. (2011). Psychotherapists' spiritual, religious, atheist or agnostic identity and their practice of psychotherapy: a grounded theory study. *Psychother Res, 21*(3), 286–303. https://doi.org/10.1080/10503307.2011.565488

Martinez, K. J. (1994). Cultural sensitivity in family therapy gone awry. *Hispanic Journal of Behavioral Sciences*, 16(1), 75–89.

McNeil, S., Pavkov, T., Hecker, L., & Killmer, J. (2012). Marriage and Family Therapy Graduate Students' Satisfaction with Training Regarding Religion and Spirituality [Article]. *Contemporary Family Therapy: An International Journal*, 34(4), 468–480. https://doi.org/10.1007/s10591-012-9205-7

Miller McInnes, M., & Van Ness Sheppard, N. (2014). What Does Spirituality Mean to You? Mapping the Spiritual Discourses of Psychotherapy Graduate Students. *Journal of spirituality in mental health*, 16(4), 286–310. https://doi.org/10.1080/19349637.2014.957605

Neden, J., Barber, J., Bradbury, G., & Cheung, A. (2011). Bringing forth spirituality dialogues in family therapy education [Article]. *Journal of Family Therapy*, 33(2), 224–228. https://doi.org/10.1111/j.1467-6427.2011.00532.x

Nordhelle, G., & Sakhi, U. S. (2019). *Angstens røtter: eksistensiell forståelse og mestring*. Fagbokforlaget.

Pargament, K. I. (2007). *Spiritually integrated psychotherapy: understanding and addressing the sacred*. Guilford Press.

Patterson, J., Hayworth, M., Turner, C., & Raskin, M. (2000). SPIRITUAL ISSUES IN FAMILY THERAPY: A GRADUATE-LEVEL COURSE [Article]. *Journal of Marital & Family Therapy*, 26(2), 199–210. http://ezproxy.diastud.no/login?url=http://search.ebscohost.com/login.aspx?direct=true&db=afh&AN=3582013&site=ehost-live

Pearson, A. (2017). Working with Religious and Spiritual Experience in Family Therapy: Manna for the Journey. *Australian and New Zealand Journal of Family Therapy*, 38(1), 43–60. https://doi.org/10.1002/anzf.1202

Satir, V. (1991). *The Satir model: family therapy and beyond*. Science and Behavior Books.

Swinton, J. (2001). *Spiritual and mental health care. Rediscovering a forgotten dimension*. Jessica Kingsley Publisher.

Telfener, U. (2017). Becoming through Belonging: The Spiritual Dimension in Psychotherapy. *Australian and New Zealand Journal of Family Therapy*, 38(1), 156–167. https://doi.org/10.1002/anzf.1199

Thayne, T. R. (1998). Opening space for clients' religious and spiritual values in therapy: A social constructionist perspective. *Journal of Family Social Work*, 2(4), 13–23.

Trimble, D. (2018). *Engaging with Spirituality in Family Therapy: Meeting in Sacred Space* (1st 2018. ed.). Cham: Springer International Publishing AG. https://doi.org/10.1007/978-3-319-77410-7

Ulland, D., & DeMarinis, V. (2014). Understanding and working with existential information in a Norwegian adolescent psychiatry context: a need and a challenge [Article]. *Mental Health, Religion & Culture*, 17(6), 582–593. https://doi.org/10.1080/13674676.2013.871241

Waldegrave, C. (2003). Grappling with a contemporary and inclusive spirituality. *Just Therapy–a Journey: A Collection of Papers from the Just Therapy Team* New Zealand Adelaide: Dulwich Centre Publications.

Walsh, F. (2003). *Normal family process: Growing diversity and complexity* (2nd ed.). Guilford Press.

Walsh, F. (2009a). Religion, spirituality, and the family: Multifaith Perspectives. In F. Walsh (Ed.), *Spiritual resources in family therapy* (2 ed., pp. 3–30). The Guildford Press.

Walsh, F. (2009b). *Spiritual resources in family therapy*. Guilford Press.

Walsh, F. (2012a). *Normal family processes: growing diversity and complexity* (4th ed.). Guilford Press.

Wendel, R. (2003). Lived Religion and Family Therapy: What Does Spirituality Have to Do with It? [Article]. *Family Process, 42*(1), 165. http://search.ebsco-host.com/login.aspx?direct=true&db=afh&AN=9407479&site=ehost-live

CHAPTER 3

Spirituality: A Multifaced Landscape

The air is full of milk and honey, but you need the senses to catch it.
—*Erik Bomann Larsen*

Many human beings seem to need meaning and connection in life. Through generations, people have prayed to higher powers or God, and many have found both strength and comfort in their faith. People's spiritual life can foster recovery and resilience (Walsh 2009). We will now take a closer look at the concept of spirituality, including a historical perspective, and see what a spiritual life may contain.

THE CONCEPT OF SPIRITUALITY

The word spirituality is rooted in the word "spirit", and in many languages, the word for spirit and breath has the same explanation. This breath of life has been described as our vital essence, that makes us feel alive. Therefore, human spirituality is closely connected to the body and is expressed in our emotions, feelings, behaviour, creativity and relationships. These powers of life help humans to find values, connections and aims in life (Grams et al. 2007).

Å. Holmberg, P. Jensen, *Working with Spirituality in Family
Systemic Practice*, Palgrave Texts in Counselling and Psychotherapy,
https://doi.org/10.1007/978-3-031-77310-5_3

Expressions of Spirituality:
Soul,
the sacred,
the existential,
meaning-making,
religion,
devoteness,
life-philosophy,
the transcendent,
faith,
values,
metaphysic love

For some people, spirituality is closely related to experiences of what makes life worth living or what makes us alive. Therefore, spiritual life might be closely connected to existential questions:

- What is life?
- Why are we here?
- What is a good life?
- Does God exist?
- Is it all over when I die? Where do I go?
- Is there a reality beyond what we can see?

Answers to these questions might help some people to find connection and direction in life. Many people have their unique spiritual journey, developed through life from birth to death. This might act as an important contributor to human satisfaction and growth in life (Miller and Thoresen 2003). As we see in the textbox, humans can have different words for their spirituality, and our task as a family therapist is to investigate the world for the specific client.

In scientific contexts, there are many definitions of spirituality. Especially in the US, the term has been much debated. This is about the relationship between spirituality and religion, and these concepts are pitted against each other. But this easily becomes a simplification as both terms are complex phenomena and multidimensional. Here there is a rich and dynamic interaction that can easily be ignored. Even if we do not define ourselves as religious, it is an acknowledgement that we are all influenced by religion to a greater or lesser extent. The secularization debate can mean that religion is portrayed in a negative light and that it is a hindrance to spiritual experiences. But even if religion can be experienced as rigid, ritualistic, and legalistic, virtually all religions are interested in spiritual perspectives (Hill and Pargament 2003).

Worthington and Sandage (2016) say spirituality is relational because it is embodied, developmental, hermeneutical and intercultural. Humans' spiritual life changes through life, both in quantity and in quality. They say spirituality always involves the brain and psychology, and spiritual experiences emerge in the context of human development, cognitive, emotional, social, moral and intercultural. Here, both attachment theory and systemic theory have a theoretical base. Our spiritual experiences are shaped and interpreted based on socio-cultural and, often, religious traditions. Relational spirituality is always influenced by contextual factors.

Cook (2004) has made a descriptive study of 265 published books and papers on spirituality and addiction. Based on this, he ended up with this definition:

> *Spirituality is a distinctive, potentially creative and universal dimension of human experience arising both within the inner subjective awareness of individuals and within communities, social groups and traditions. It may be experienced as relationship with that which is intimately 'inner', immanent and personal, within the self and others, and/or as relationship with that which is wholly 'other', transcendent and beyond the self. It is experienced as being of fundamental or ultimate importance and is thus concerned with matters of meaning and purpose in life, truth and values.* (p. 548)

Cock says there is a need to further research to consider how these aspects of spirituality are managed in the practice of treatment and says there are ethical issues to be addressed concerning the problems that arise when the spiritualities of therapist and client are discordant.

HUMANISTIC SPIRITUALITY

As systemic therapists, we embrace a humanistic spirituality which goes beyond religion, which means we are not concerned with what separates us, but rather what unites us. We all have something to learn of each other.

We prefer a more cosmic we, where we look through a cosmic lens, where the love for oneself and others is the driving force. Love is a paradox and involves a clear decision, a flow of energy that is willingly exchanged and allowed without demanding payment in return.

We often have limited constructions of spirituality and religion created by our culture, traditions and experiences and acknowledge that spiritual wisdom is far greater than we can comprehend. Spiritual wisdom is more a synthesis than analysis, more paradoxical than linear, more a dance than a march. We prefer non-dualistic thinking with the ability to read the moment with a non-judgmental and exclusionary attitude. If there are parts we do not understand, we will live things open—and let them speak to us (Rohr 2014).

History of the Concept

Across cultures and millennia, humans have searched for meaning and connectedness, prayed to a higher power or God, or seen their lives from a larger perspective (Paloutzian and Park 2013). We are more than biology, and despite great progress scientifically, we need something more that science cannot fill.

Originally, spirituality in the West was a term from the Catholic church about how to nurture the soul. In the English language, the word spirituality was used for the first time in 1441, with the meaning "The body of spiritual and ecclesiastical persons". In other words, not for everyone. Spirituality was hardly used outside religious circles. Spirituality was a discipline within the Catholic clergy and was later linked to Christian spirituality, being filled with the Spirit of God and living one's faith in daily life (Sheldrake 2007). This was a time when the church had great power, and it was a huge split between the spiritual and the secular (Rizzutto 2009). First, in the early 1900s, the concept lost some of its accusing meaning and the term became more descriptive.

The concept of spirituality has had a great development, both in scope and in content. From the 1960s, the term was used in many religious contexts, often associated with mysticism and contemplation. In recent decades, spirituality has often been used based on a more subjective and individual spirituality, often with limited impact on religiosity (Heelas 2008; Laugerud 2012)

From the 1980s, several faiths in the West were characterized as "spirituality". There was a decrease in support of traditional religious institutions, a more general cultural pluralism and an increase in individualized forms of expressions of faith (Ulland 2012). Although the term is used to an increasing extent within traditional religious contexts, it is in the alternative spiritual environment that we see the greatest development. A wide range of journals and books have been published and many conferences, both nationally and internationally, have taken place (Olsen 2006). We have a comprehensive alternative medicine and healing business, which, together with "new religions", participates in the development of self-development, and spiritual and meditative practices (Ulland 2012). The church no longer controls people, and many find ways to nourish their souls. Our postmodern society questions our basic assumptions about knowledge and religion, and it is a recognition that our ideological and religious constructs are tied to history and context.

A Spiritual Life

The spiritual life is about ontology, about being, and the relationship to the non-material, that which we do not fully understand. It connects to the abstract and absolute in life, death and our existence. It is about ideological conviction, faith or philosophy of life. This again shows itself in aspirations, life dreams, view of people and view of the world. We might see ourselves in a larger perspective (Serrander 2018).

In a holistic view, most people are spiritual, but they can reflect on it to a greater or lesser degree. When people are in crisis, becoming seriously ill or old, the spiritual perspective often emerges more strongly. Miller and Thoresen (2003) says:

> *Everyone has their unique spiritual journey developed through life from birth to death, which acts as an important contributor to human satisfaction and growth in life.*

The Scottish professor John Swinton (2001) says being spiritual has three perspectives:

1. A universal human dimension
2. Linked to culture, history and social relationships
3. Something unique for the one, that nobody else has

The spiritual life is not a static state, but a journey with many stops throughout life. This means that the experiences and opinions we had in childhood will be able to lower themselves quite radically throughout life. We might mirror life's experiences in our spiritual lives. We will keep something, discard something else and maybe something new will be included. Perhaps some become more concerned with this as we get older. At an early age, we have to establish an identity, a home, relationships, friends, a community, and security, building a platform for our only life. Maybe we then have less space to include spiritual perspectives. However, it will probably depend a lot on what we experience in our way of life.

As we get older, we see that things that were important before may not matter as much anymore. We realize that we are not immortal, and many people find that life goes by quickly. We meet stumbling stones, suffering and also deep joy on our journey. Getting in touch with our spiritual life can create awakening, healing and growth. Something that can in turn create good ripple effects for others, nature and the world. Spiritual wisdom is a way of being, fully open to a knowing that is more than rational thoughts alone. To see in such a way is to keep all inner spaces open—mind, heart, and body—all at once. When paying respectful and non-egoic attention to humans' spiritual lives, the unexpected and supernatural can happen (Rohr 2013).

Supernatural Experiences

Speaking of supernatural experiences, which are often referred to as "exceptional human experiences", is a collective term for mystical, spiritual or unusual experiences. These are experiences that can be difficult to explain, and which can be positive, but also negative. You may have experienced this yourself in one form or another. Research shows that this is something that millions of people around the world experience, and it can have a major existential impact on the person. For almost a century, psychiatry has treated these experiences as pathology, and this practice is seen as outdated and unreflective, based on a reductionist view of humanity (Swinton 2020). People have the experiences that they have, and we must rather explore what is contained in those subjective experiences. As therapists, we should be open to exploring what this means for clients, and how this affects them.

SPIRITUALITY AND THE CHURCH

Concerning the church, in Northern Europe, there has been a Lutheran dominance since the middle of the sixteenth century. This doctrine has created an ontological distinction between the divine, eternal and temporal (Aadnanes 2012). This split, dualism, has probably been a contributor to the distinction between secular and religious practice, between more secular psychotherapy and pastoral care. It seems to have contributed to a further specialization of professional practice and an elimination of the holistic perspective on humanity. Having spiritual challenges, you visit priests and pastoral counsellors. With mental issues or relational problems, you go to a psychologist or other therapists. This division makes it not natural to talk about spiritual perspectives in therapeutic contexts (Sheehan et al. 2007). And even worse, if you don't want to involve church leaders in your spiritual life, where do you go for help?

As we interpret the Protestant movement, there has been a lot of focus on the Word, the right doctrine, and a theological framework. The earlier churches seemed to be much more concerned with the body, not just something "for the head". "The lived body" (Merleau-Ponty 2012) is a part of the spiritual life and has to be connected to spiritual experiences and practices. If a religious spirituality reduces our spiritual journey to following the right teachings, we can have a shift from something interpersonal to impersonal. This has also been a result of the Enlightenment, where *trust* in God was changed to *faith* in God (Benner 2011).

WESTERN SOCIETY OF TODAY

The last few decades, in the Western world, have been called a postmodern era. This is characterized by a great diversity, where people must find their own meaning and shape their lives, connected to relevant communities. For humans, the church can give a sense of belonging and stability, something to hold on to, in all the life changes. At the same time, many felt that the church violated people's freedom, dignity and autonomy, something that had to be fought and overcome in order to regain true humanity (Engedal 2004).

With our digital development, the world has become small and vulnerable. The horrors of the world enter the living room, natural disasters become obvious to us and we understand that if we are to survive, we must learn to practice wholeness, coherence and solidarity in a completely new way. This can create uneasiness and uncertainty, and time, seen in the context of the world, suddenly becomes very short. Although we have witnessed incredible advances in science and technology, we have also seen an evil and destructiveness that is difficult to understand.

Maybe it is not so strange that people can feel existential unrest. Who am I in the middle of all this? Knowledge in science and the possibilities of reason to produce objective, reliable and universally valid knowledge have been shaken. Various philosophies and theories have undressed and decon-structed the science of modernity. A new understanding has emerged where all knowledge is historically conditioned and contextually rooted. Our epistemology is both rooted and limited in the language and culture we live in. This can be experienced as liberating, but also demanding. What was certain in the past can now be problematic.

The church has in many ways lost its monopoly; the individual's free-dom of choice, diversity and tolerance are emphasized as an overriding value. But this also creates challenges, and we can stand in the gap between fragmentation and destructive fundamentalism. This is perhaps one of the reasons why more people seem to be concerned with the spiritual; there is a longing for something more and bigger. Perhaps this is a reaction to overburdened individuals who cannot bear to carry all choices, informa-tion, all ambiguities in postmodern culture on their shoulders. In this landscape, various challenges can arise related to identity and self-esteem, relational distress, existential homelessness and spiritual longing (Engedal 2004).

People of today have a lot of choice possibilities. Society is multicul-tural; for many, the world is wide open. We are taught early on to reflect critically; we have to find our own opinion. In our society, we see a suspi-cion against established religions. Perhaps most Christianity. In a Western context, Christianity is the religion we know the best and many have a relationship to. It forces the individual to reflect on, "What is spirituality for me?" When external authorities diminish, the individual is forced to become more reflective and ask themselves what they believe in—and why they believe what they believe. Here, people need to be met seriously with their experiences in a context that is elastic, tentative and permissive. Many have a belief or a philosophy of life that is more inductive, that is, based on soulful experience and feelings, rather than a deductive interpretation with established truths (Geels et al. 2006).

Critics say that if everything is relative and unreliable, this will create an identity crisis, an eroding culture and identity. In the society of today, we already see the consequences with a large number of psychological problems and a lot of rootless people. If people do not know what to look for, it can create socio-cultural poverty. This in turn can create meaninglessness and confusion with a lost identity (DeMarinis 2008).

All professional development is based on science, research and experience. Implicitly here we find our view of life, something that will show in the practical practice of the profession. Our view of life contains a human view, a perception of reality and a view of values, something which can again be said to give us answers to our existential questions. Our perception of reality says something about the origin of the world, the creation of meaning and death. Our view of humanity is something about what we experience a human being to be, whether there is a difference between humans and animals and whether humans are fundamentally good. Our view of values is concerned with what is right or wrong, good or bad and whether values are absolute or relative (Aadnanes 2012).

AN ECOLOGICAL PERSPECTIVE INCLUDES SPIRITUALITY

As humans, we are connected to all living things. We are part of the universe. The word universe means all existing matter and space considered as we call the cosmos.

The word ecology is named as the study of the relationships between living organisms, including humans, and their physical environment.

This network of life consists of many relationships; we are part of plants, animals and microorganisms. This household of the earth has an inherent ability to sustain life. As members of this global community of living beings, we should help sustain life. This is ecological sustainability. Feeling a connectedness to nature has been linked to decreased stress, better connections with other people and a heightened sense of purpose and oneness with the world.

Capra and Luisi (2016) say our behaviour should respect human dignity and basic human rights. As living beings, we are all dependent on each other. The world is an integrated whole. The deepest essence of ecological consciousness is therefore spiritual.

This will affect our thinking and values. Capra and Luisi say instead of being assertive, we can be integrative, strive to think more non-linearly and rather more holistically, intuitively and see life more as a synthesis. This will make us more concerned with collaboration, quality, and partnership, and preserving—more than expanding.

This thinking and values have historically been difficult, especially for men, who often have gained power. In a systemic ecological paradigm, we would rather help people gain power over themselves. One man who can be a good example is the Brazilian pedagogue, Paulo Freire (1979). He says that we all participate in moving systems and believes that we must all take the initiative to improve and change our world for the better. He says a dialogue in love is an existential necessity. It requires courage, humility, hope and belief in humans, but also critical thinking. He says, "Critical thinking is in opposition to naive thinking" (p. 76), and claims the existential value of true solidarity only exists in practice. Freire says, "The more active people take part in the examination of their themes, the stronger they deepen their critical alertness to reality" (p. 92). Cultures can develop myths that people internalize, which in turn can give a narrow view of reality. As cultural bearers, we can be both oppressors and liberators.

Gregory Bateson (1979) wanted us to learn of nature and see life as dynamic and part of the whole. Having a circular perspective on the relation between people and the world, everything and everyone lives in relation to each other. We have to meet people in their context. Thinking systemically is a way of seeing and acting and appreciating complexity. This also includes spirituality. To be systemic is to naturally adopt a spiritual focus. Bateson called it the sacred, built on humility and curiosity (Bateson and Bateson 2005). A spiritual stance in systemic therapy can embrace a diversity of epistemologies and spiritual belief systems. The question is whether we are open to and listen for it (Larner 2017).

What Can We Learn from the Nature?

Bateson was in many ways ahead of his time. He believed that industrial development was destructive for us humans, our relation to something bigger was destroyed. This is perhaps something we see today when many young people speak up to protect our nature and yearn to live a simpler life. Eco philosophy has grown out of environmental activism, which says that we are completely dependent on our ecosystem (Næss and Haukeland 2008). As humans, we are incredibly vulnerable and completely dependent on nature and the world as a whole. We are part of the nature.

By focusing on people's dependence on nature, ecopsychology was developed in the 1970s. In the cooling water of this came ecotherapy, where nature is invited into the therapeutic relationship and in the therapeutic work. The body has a central function here, and sight, hearing, smell, touch, feeling and movement are all important. Ulrika Ernvik, a Swedish family therapist, says that the therapist should first explore his own relationship with nature, what she calls your ecological self and also your ecological history (Ernvik 2022). How a concrete worker should be adapted to those who come and what makes sense for the individual therapist, but what is common is that nature is inculcated in the therapeutic work of change. It is also a belief that nature itself can contribute to a healing process. A deeper relationship with nature will create a deeper relationship with ourselves. It is about being able to experience nature through the whole body, feeling that we are part of nature, and finally experiencing that our thoughts will expand.

Richard Rohr (2018), a Franciscan priest and writer, says the world is the locus of the sacred and provides all the metaphors that the soul needs for its growth. He thinks God has been revealing God's love, goodness and beauty since the very beginning through the natural world of creation, and cite the Bible: "God looked at everything God had made and found it very good" (Genesis 1:31). In this, all things have its place. He even goes so far as to say that the reason we humans so often need therapy is that we have removed ourselves from nature. He says that nature, God's creation, is the primary "bible". He says that nature speaks to us and says we belong to each other, we are connected, you matter. All living things have souls. A lesson from the natural world is a lesson from the divine.

The Norwegian authors and therapists Sakhi and Nordhelle (2021) say that there is much healing in nature. Here we find ancient wisdom. They say we are part of nature, but we have to open ourselves to it. They encourage us to try to put aside the difficulties and focus on the sensory impressions that nature gives us. Plants, animals and people need growing conditions in harmony with nature. No organism lives in isolation. Sakhi and Nordhelle say that it is not possible to speed up the ripening of an apple that grows naturally. They say we humans are often impatient and try to force what we want before the time is right. If we don't accept that we have to wait, we are acting against nature. When we don't force things, they will naturally fall into place. Listening inward is like listening to our inner nature. The better contact we have with ourselves, the easier it will be to follow nature's principles.

> **Spiritual Messengers**
> Birds, animals and nature itself can be experienced as spiritual messengers. A woman told about the memorial service for their deceased son. They sat outside, and when they sang a song, a bird sat on a pole and sang with them. Several of the seals noticed the bird. When they stopped singing, it flew away, but at the next song, it came back and sang along again. What was this? It felt like a greeting from the other side, now the son had found peace.

Spiritual Sources in Human Life

As we have seen, nature can be a huge spiritual source in humans' life. Spirituality seems to be an important life force that undergirds, motivates and vitalizes humans' existence. Swinton (2001) says:

> *Spirituality is an intra, inter and transpersonal experience that is shaped and directed by the experiences of the individuals and of the communities within which they live out their lives. … Spirituality is a human activity that attempts to express these profound experiences and inner logics in terms that are meaningful for individuals.* (p. 20)

Humans' spiritual life has many sources. There are great cultural and traditional differences related to spirituality in our world, but at the same time, there are some factors that seem to be common to humanity: the need for love and belonging. However, humans nourish their souls in different ways. It can be related to music, art, prayer, meditation or a relation to a higher power, like God Allah. People can be religious, but not aware of their spirituality. People can also be spiritual but not religious.

As systemic therapists, we can help clients to identify their spiritual sources, the current, the past or what they are longing for. Some spiritual sources can cause distress and discomfort; others may be a way of coping, healing and resilience. As therapists we can help clients reconnect with what they find meaningful in their lives, what fits their values and preferences and what nourishes their souls.

Spiritual sources can be found both inside or outside organized societies and can include:

- Contemplative practice (prayer, meditation)
- Rituals
- Relationship with God or a Higher Power
- Involvement in faith community
- Communion with nature and animals
- Creative art
- Service to others, social activism
- Intimate bonds and connections. (Walsh 2012)

As therapists, we can cultivate empathy and compassion, listening deeply and being open for spiritual issues. To fully listen to other reflections and experiences is difficult, especially if we experience this differently, alien and perhaps even wrong. If we take others' perspectives into account bodily and try to feel and reflect on the other perspectives, it can help us be with the other. A loving attitude where we look for the good, what gives life and meaning can also be a help on the way.

Another word for spiritual sources can be spiritual needs. In Chap. 1, we have described spiritual needs from a Danish study (Stripp et al. 2023). In addition, Hodge and Horvath (2011) from the US have identified and described in a Qualitative Meta-Synthesis, six spiritual needs from clients in Health Care Settings:

1. Meaning, purpose and hope
2. Relationship with God
3. Spiritual practice
4. Religious obligations
5. Interpersonal connection
6. Professional staff interactions

In clients' lived experience, these needs were often intertwined.

Spiritual needs change with time and circumstances, depending on which sources we find important and what kind of challenges we face in life. Spiritual needs are at the heart of our well-being, helping us to live a more harmonious life—in the middle of everything. Research shows that such kind of care can help overcome fear and anxiety, and be health-promoting for the clients (Borge and Mæland 2017). However, there is no "one size fits all", we are all influenced by culture, traditions and experiences, but we can still find some common denominators for what we call spirituality.

The spiritual seems to be something we exercise and experience. Spirituality can form human ethics and values and help to find direction and coherence in life. The spirituality of humans can give a sense of wholeness, harmony and connection with others, nature and the universe. Therefore, eco-thinking, peace, justice and solidarity can be deeply spiritual questions (Canda and Furman 2010; Jeong Woong and Canda 2010).

Research says that spirituality is an important health-promoting perspective (Koenig et al. 2012). Still, we know that people have experiences for good and for bad. Experiences that affect life in different ways. Systemic work is a comprehensive relational thinking where both problems and solutions can be found in physical, mental, social, cultural and spiritual perspectives.

PROBLEMATIC SPIRITUALITY

Not all spirituality is health-promoting. We can be trapped in a system that creates coercion, lack of freedom, anxiety and oppression. The main element of spirituality has to be in the service of becoming deeply human. Benner (2011) says we are not going to be angels or Gods or some form of supernatural beings. Spiritual practices and paths that distance us from our vitality or what it means to be human can leave us impoverished and diminished.

Benner says that spirituality moves us away from life when it distances us from our bodies:

> *The body anchors the spiritual and the mental, grounding perceptions in sensations, feelings in emotion, thoughts in action, defences in muscles, and beliefs in behaviour.* (p. 5)

People can still believe in God, or maybe sometimes pray, but will find their way. Spiritual journeys might be shaped by our longings. Being in contact with our inner life, our passions should be accepted and known. Through this, we might be released from the prisons of mind and come back to our senses. It can help us to be fully alive, free us from the small life of ego, allowing us to have a more peaceful life with ourselves, others and the world. It can help us be more open to the mystery of life (Benner 2011).

Struggling with the Religion

Betty and Carl had been together since they were teenagers. They were members of the Mormon church. They married early, in the church, without knowing each other very well, and the relationship was difficult from the start. The congregation affected the view of the family, child-rearing and finances, to name a few. Now, Betty had signed out because she could no longer stand for the congregation's belief. Carl found this very difficult. He had an active role in the congregation. He had spoken to the leadership about their problems and supported what the leadership thought about it. Betty experienced this as a big betrayal. The marriage was in a major crisis. According to the doctrine, the family was supposed to be together after death, in eternity. Betty had struggled with her faith and the church's requirements and rules since she was little. She never felt good enough, neither for God, the congregation or Carl. The family was expected to come together to church every Sunday, which Betty could no longer bear. The couple struggled with closeness, both sexually and emotionally, and had isolated themselves from family and networks.

RELIGIOUS SPIRITUALITY

Religion is an important source for many people in their spiritual life. Religion comes from the Latin word "Religare", which means "to connect, to bind", a bond between humanity or a power greater than human beings. It is a relationship between God and a higher being. The definition of religion often refers to formal systems of belief and belonging to a religious group or community, usually including a God or a higher power. The various religions provide values and guidelines for life (Swinton 2001; Walsh 2013).

It may be important to note that the word spirit, which we define as breath, in religious contexts can have two parts, both God's Spirit and the continuous gift of life. Breathing might exemplify the Divine Presence within each human. These might be the person's most essential dignity. Every breath is a reminder of God's presence and affirms the God-given value of each person's spirit. It is an expression of the Holy Breath seeking to find freedom in our world (Saint-Jean 2022).

Scientists and sociologists have prophesied the downfall of religion, but as the world has evolved, it has not lost its relevance. Today it is said that the West has become a post-secular society, where religion has not lost its power but is coming back with renewed force (Habermas 2008). Postmodern society is characterized by a relativistic mindset that everyone must find their truth. Many people need something to hold on to, something to lean on in storms, something bigger than themselves. The religious appeal lies in the idea that God or the Universe touches us. It is a practice of relation. Praying, for example, is both listening and responding. The German sociologist Helmut Rosa (2019) calls it "deep resonance", "there is one who hears you, who understands you, who can find ways and means of reaching you and responding to you" (p. 261). It is the promise that the universe of God still speaks even when we are incapable of hearing it. One idea is to believe that in every human soul, there is a glimpse of God. Perhaps religion is about being able to set boundaries in a relatively limitless society, and see our limitations. The Canadian writer Stephen Jenkinson (2015) says he thinks boundaries are an important part of the religious life. All over the world, humans have rituals and time for prayer and praise, sacred time and different traditions for life and death. Maybe religion is like a container for the human, moral and biological boundaries of which "secular" modernity has lost its understanding.

Most religions have an overarching idea of charity, reciprocity and justice built into their ethics and legal system. The "golden rule" is an example of that. However, there are also examples of religions that can block the spiritual world, which acts oppressively and closes human rights. If love is the most important element in religion, it must create a universe of hope, nourishment and liberation for the human soul. Being a good religious person does not necessarily mean you are on a spiritual journey. Being a religious person does not necessarily make you a good human being. A commitment to religious practice does not always produce a life-enhancing spirituality (Benner 2011). However, the message of most religions is that God or a Higher Power depends on us to protect ourselves and be nurturing, loving and protective against other people.

As family therapists, we need to know that religion can be important for many clients. We also have to know that being a Christian for example, there are as many variations as there is faith, also within the individual family. If God is an important relationship for the client, for strength and help on the path of life, we should face this with curiosity and openness.

McGilchrist (2021) believe God is far more accessible to heart and soul than the intellect. If God is the source behind all that exists and the centre of all being, it is a mystery, greater than thought can capture. However, if we know everything, there is no room for anything to grow. Gilchrist says science is a matter of knowledge, religion is a matter of knowing—by experience. Faith can never be certain; doubt is a necessary part of faith. However, religion constantly reminds us of a larger context, an obligation to other humans, to the earth and the universe.

Non-religious Spirituality

If we believe that being spiritual is part of being human, there are of course many who are spiritual without being religious. Even though we are all influenced by religion, many people do not find religion relevant to their life. It does not mean they are not spiritual, but they find other sources than the churches, mosques and religious life can offer.

Helminiak (2001) argues that spirituality is a human phenomenon independent of personal religion or belief in God, not a perspective just to include in big crises but a natural part of all human. He criticizes the idea that talking about spirituality often is about religion or a faith in God. Spirituality is a dimension of human experience that includes values, attitudes, beliefs and emotions which exists in all humans.

Elkins (1999) advocate a more humanistic and phenomenological spirituality outside traditional religion. He says spirituality is based on the belief that there are two dimensions of reality, the material and the nonmaterial. In the nonmaterial dimension, we anchor our life and find our values and meaning. Spirituality is expressed as a way of being and experiencing through the awareness of a transcendent dimension characterized by values in regard to self, others, nature, life and what humans consider to be "the ultimate". Elkin says as a spiritual person, you believe in more than you can see, and life is deeply meaningful and has a purpose. They are also concerned with the sacredness of life, altruism and idealism, the idea of a mission in life and also not being controlled by material values. This calls for a greater contact and closeness with people's souls.

If clients are not religious and even do not think of themselves as "spiritual", it is still important to explore how they—or might they—find strength, meaning connection, and nourishment in facing life challenges. What beliefs and practices could support their resilience, bolster their efforts and strengthen their bonds? It is also important to respect atheists' nonbelief in God or an afterlife, exploring their views of a meaningful life and fulfilling relationships. What feels right for a person today may be something else tomorrow. la Cour et al. (2012) underpins this:

The divide between them is artificial and counterproductive for relevant research in the field. When concepts are not adequately delimited and defined, and when close traditions seem to ignore each other, then the opportunities for grasping the rich clinical reality of meaning-making in the experience of medical conditions are reduced. In the real world, patients may think about existence in secular, in spiritual and in religious terms, and a majority do so simultaneously. In their minds these currents may separate, may shift position and may fuse at different times during the course of their life. Reality is multilayered, and investigation, theory and research should reflect this. (p. 8)

When reality is multilayered, therapists should meet the clients or the families with openness and curiosity and be able to listen and understand their life and their practice.

Reflections

1. Write down all the words you can think of that relate to spirituality. Choose the word that is closest to you. Rewrite that word for five minutes without using the word itself. Finally, reflect on what this means to you.
2. How do you nourish your soul?
3. Go for a walk in the forest. Listen to the sounds you find there, the smell, the tones and colours, sounds and the rhythms. When you get home, write down your experiences in a book. Repeat this and continue typing. When you have repeated this ten times, read your text and write a meta-reflection on your texts. Then start over.
4. Write your story related to religion. What are your reflections or feelings?
5. Read the Bible text slowly about Moses and the burning bush.
   [1] Now Moses was tending the flock of Jethro his father-in-law, the priest of Midian, and he led the flock to the far side of the wilderness and came to Horeb, the mountain of God.
   [2] There the angel of the LORD appeared to him in flames of fire from within a bush. Moses saw that though the bush was on fire it did not burn up.
   [3] So Moses thought, "I will go over and see this strange sight—why the bush does not burn up."
   [4] When the LORD saw that he had gone over to look, God called to him from within the bush, "Moses! Moses!"
   And Moses said, "Here I am."
   [5] "Do not come any closer," God said. "Take off your sandals, for the place where you are standing is holy ground."
   [6] Then he said, "I am the God of your father,[a] the God of Abraham, the God of Isaac and the God of Jacob." At this, Moses hid his face, because he was afraid to look at God.
   - What does the text say to you?
   - Do you have had extraordinary experiences by yourself?
   - How would you react if a client of yours told you a story like this?
6. What was important to you before, but not important now? What is important to you now that wasn't important before?
7. Which people have been decisive for you in your spiritual development?

References

Bateson, G. (1979). *Mind and nature: a necessary unity.* Wildwood House.

Bateson, G., & Bateson, M. C. (2005). *Angels fear: towards an epistemology of the sacred.* Hampton press.

Benner, D. G. (2011). *Soulful spirituality: becoming fully alive and deeply human.* Brazos Press.

Borge, L., & Mæland, E. (2017). Er det rom for livssynstemaer i dagens psykisk helsearbeid? *Klinisk Sygepleje, 31*(03), 165–177. http://www.idunn.no/klinisk_sygepleje/2017/03/er_det_rom_for_livssynstemaer_idagens_psykisk_helsearbeid

Canda, E. R., & Furman, L. D. (2010). *Spiritual diversity in social work practice* (2nd ed.). Oxford University Press.

Capra, F., & Luisi, P. L. (2016). *Liv, system, helhed: det levende som system: en syntese.* Forlaget Mindspace.

Cook, C. C. H. (2004). Addiction and spirituality. *Addiction, 99*(5), 539–551. https://doi.org/10.1111/j.1360-0443.2004.00715.x

DeMarinis, V. (2008). The impact of postmodernization on existential health in Sweden: Psychology of religion's function in existential public health analysis. *Archive for the Psychology of Religion, 30*(1), 57–74.

Elkins, D. N. (1999). *Beyond religion: a personal program for building a spiritual life outside the walls of traditional religion.* Quest Books, Theosophical Publ.

Engedal, L. G. (2004). Kristen sjelesorg i en postmoderne kultur: utfordringer og muligheter. In (pp. 19–72). Verbum.

Ernvik, U. (2022). *Ekopsykoterapi: psykoterapi i och med naturen för vuxna och barn* (Upplaga 1. ed.). Studentlitteratur.

Freire, P. (1979). *Pedagogy of the oppressed.* Sheed and Ward.

Geels, A., Wikström, O., Hermanson, J., & Junus, P. (2006). *Den religiösa människan: en introduktion till religionspsykologin* ([5. omarb. utg.]. ed.). Natur och Kultur.

Grams, W., Carlson, T., & McGeorge, C. (2007). Integrating Spirituality into Family Therapy Training: An Exploration of Faculty Members' Beliefs [Article]. *Contemporary Family Therapy: An International Journal, 29*(3), 147–161. https://doi.org/10.1007/s10591-007-9042-2

Habermas, J. (2008). Notes on a post-secular society. *Revista colombiana de sociología* (31), 169–183.

Heelas, P. (2008). *Spiritualities of life: New Age romanticism and consumptive capitalism.* Blackwell Publ.

Helminiak, D. A. (2001). Treating Spiritual Issues in Secular Psychotherapy [Article]. *Counseling & Values, 45*(3), 163. http://search.ebscohost.com/login.aspx?direct=true&db=afh&AN=4427875&site=ehost-live

Hill, P. C., & Pargament, K. I. (2003). Advances in the conceptualization and measurement of religion and spirituality. Implications for physical and mental health research. *Am Psychol, 58*(1), 64–74.

Hodge, D. R., & Horvath, V. E. (2011). Spiritual Needs in Health Care Settings: A Qualitative Meta-Synthesis of Clients' Perspectives [Article]. *Social Work, 56*(4), 306–316. http://search.ebscohost.com/login.aspx?direct=true&db=af h&AN=69822099&site=ehost-live

Jenkinson, S. (2015). *Die wise: a manifesto for sanity and soul.* North Atlantic Books.

Jeong Woong, C., & Canda, E. R. (2010). The Meaning and Engagement of Spirituality for Positive Youth Development in Social Work [Article]. *Families in Society, 91*(2), 121–126. https://doi.org/10.1606/1044-3894.3981

Koenig, King D. E., & Carson, V. B. (2012). *Handbook of religion and health* (2nd ed.). Oxford University Press.

la Cour, P., Ausker, N. H., & Hvidt, N. C. (2012). Six Understandings of the Word 'Spirituality' in a Secular Country. *Archive for the Psychology of Religion, 34*(1), 63–81. https://doi.org/10.1163/157361212X649634

Larner, G. (2017). Spiritual Dialogues in Family Therapy. *Australian and New Zealand Journal of Family Therapy, 38*(1), 125–141. https://doi.org/10.1002/anzf.1207

Laugerud, T. (2012). Kirken i møte med åndelige erfaringer i grenseland til kristen tro. *Tidsskrift for praktisk teologi, 1.*

McGilchrist, I. (2021). *The matter with things: our brains, our delusions and the unmaking of the world.* Perspectiva Press.

Merleau-Ponty, M. (2012). Phenomenology of perception. In. Routledge.

Miller, W. R., & Thoresen, C. E. (2003). Spirituality, religion, and health. An emerging research field. *Am Psychol, 58*(1), 24–35.

Næss, A., & Haukeland, P. I. (2008). *Life's philosophy: reason & feeling in a deeper world.* University of Georgia Press.

Olsen, H. (2006). *Spiritualitet: en ny dimensjon i religionsforskningen* (Vol. nr 127). Høgskolen i Agder.

Paloutzian, R. F., & Park, C. L. (2013). *Handbook of the psychology of religion and spirituality* (2nd ed.). Guilford Press.

Rizzutto, A.-M. (2009). Psychoanalytic considerations about spiritually oriented psychotherapy In L. Sperry & E. P. Shafranske (Eds.), *Spiritually oriented psychotherapy* (pp. 31–50). American Psychological Association.

Rohr, R. (2013). *Immortal diamond: the search for our true self.* SPCK.

Rohr, R. (2014). *Eager to love: the alternative way of Francis of Assisi.* Franciscan Media.

Rohr, R. (2018). *Richard Rohr: essential teachings on love.* ORBIS books.

Rosa, H. (2019). *Resonance: a sociology of our relationship to the world.* Polity.

Saint-Jean, P. (2022). *The crucible of racism: Ignatian spirituality and the power of hope.* Orbis Books.

Sakhi, U. S., & Nordhelle, G. (2021). *Å leve i pakt med Moder jord: integral terapi* (1. utgave. ed.). Cappelen Damm.

Serrander, E. (2018). När kroppen visar vägen. In D. Stiwne (Ed.), *Existens och psykisk hälsa* (pp. 65–87). Studentlitteratur.

Sheehan, J., Flaskas, C., & McCarthy, I. (2007). *Hope and despair in narrative and family therapy: adversity, forgiveness, and reconciliation.* Routledge.

Sheldrake, P. (2007). *A brief history of spirituality.* Blackwell Publ.

Stripp, T. A., Wehberg, S., Büssing, A., Koenig, H. G., Balboni, T. A., VanderWeele, T. J., Søndergaard, J., & Hvidt, N. C. (2023). Spiritual needs in Denmark: a population-based cross-sectional survey linked to Danish national registers. *The Lancet Regional Health–Europe, 28.*

Swinton, J. (2001). *Spiritual and mental health care. Rediscovering a forgotten dimension.* Jessica Kingsley Publisher.

Swinton, J. (2020). *Finding Jesus in the storm: the spiritual lives of Christians with mental health challenges.* William. B. Eerdmans Publishing Company.

Ulland, D. (2012). Embodied spirituality. https://doi.org/10.1163/157361 212X645340

Walsh, F. (2009). Religion, spirituality, and the family: Multifaith Perspectives. In F. Walsh (Ed.), *Spiritual resources in family therapy* (2 ed., pp. 3–30). The Guildford Press.

Walsh, F. (2012). *Normal family processes: growing diversity and complexity* (4th ed.). Guilford Press.

Walsh, F. (2013). Religion and spirituality: A family systems perspective in clinical practice. In K. I. Pargament, A. Mahoney, & E. P. Shafranske (Eds.), *APA Handbook of Psychology, Religion and Spirituality* (Vol. 2, pp. 189–205). American Psychological Association.

Worthington, E. L., & Sandage, S. J. (2016). *Forgiveness and spirituality in psychotherapy: A relational approach.* American Psychological Association. https://doi.org/10.1037/14712-000

Aadnanes, P. M. (2012). *Livssyn* (4. utg. ed.). Universitetsforl.

CHAPTER 4

Spirituality in Intercultural Family Therapy

We may have different religions, different languages, and different
coloured skin, but we all belong to one human race.
—*Kofi Annan*

INTRODUCTION

Intercultural communication implies achieving common understandings
and breaking some codes in our encounter with unfamiliar cultures. In
this chapter, we will explore communication in intercultural encounters
where different forms of spirituality form part of the dialogue. In this
chapter, spirituality is mainly described and exemplified as religion. We
will emphasize how we can understand different forms of communication
and professional encounters in which culture, religion and gender are
important.

Å. Holmberg, P. Jensen, *Working with Spirituality in Family
Systemic Practice*, Palgrave Texts in Counselling and Psychotherapy,
https://doi.org/10.1007/978-3-031-77310-5_4

Intercultural Communication

Intercultural communication deals with the relationship and communication between different cultures, and how people can understand each other across cultural barriers. This process involves the exchange and interpretation of signs and messages between people who see themselves as representatives of cultural groups. The people are so different that this affects the meanings they ascribe to various elements of their culture. Intercultural communication is a group phenomenon experienced by individuals.

Culture is a complex concept, defined in different ways within various traditions, and there has been much discussion of diverse definitions of the concept of culture. Culture implies the ideas common to a group about what is right and wrong, ugly and beautiful, everyday behaviour and the meaning of life (Aasen 2012). "Culture deals with systems of knowledge, values and meanings that people use to orientate themselves in the world" (Vike and Eide 2009). This definition implies that there is, for example, a Western culture, an African culture and a Pakistani culture. Within such large cultures, we can find many smaller subcultures (subgroups within the culture), such as various religious cultures, urban and rural cultures, northern English culture, political cultures and youth cultures. There also appears to be a broader youth culture with common features linked to music and clothes that crosses the boundaries of national cultures.

In this book, we therefore operate with a descriptive rather than a normative concept of culture. Our analytical approach does not involve a normative perspective, where we judge a culture based on our own norms or values about what is right and wrong. In a descriptive approach, the aim is instead to try to understand cultural features from within, and to examine the significance of certain phenomena and forms of expression in the context in which they occur. Diversity in ways of understanding reality is a key aspect of a pluralistic society. Pluralism is the coexistence of various outlooks on life, where people with different views and interpretations of life and the world can live together.

At the same time, we can maintain a dynamic concept of culture where we continuously reinterpret the world in our encounters with others. We come into being with others, and we may belong to different cultural groups, and thus be bearers of a distinctive mixture of cultural characteristics, while the culture of groups also changes in encounters with others. "Culture is the changeable common set of opinions that is established and changed time and time again when people do something together" (Eriksen 2021, p. 25). In order to understand a multicultural society, we can benefit from both a descriptive and a dynamic concept of culture. A descriptive concept may be best suited to comprehend the distinctive features of cultures, while a dynamic concept of culture can make us aware of changes.

DISCONTINUITY BETWEEN INDIVIDUAL AND GROUP

Discontinuity
Discontinuity implies a lack of connection between two levels such as the group level and the individual level. If I only know one Swede, I cannot say that I know what Swedes are like. One member of the group cannot represent the whole group.

Much knowledge presented about culture, religions, views of life, denominations and spiritual activity is most meaningful at the group level. This is generally common knowledge among the members of a group. It may be knowledge of beliefs and rituals, of how to understand reality and of different practices that are typical of the group. For example, Muslims and Christians have slightly different eating habits and different prayer routines or the lack of them. In addition, within these communities there may be groups with different practices and beliefs. Groups and congregations are more or less open to different views and practices. In Norway, only a few years ago it was difficult or impossible for a priest to have a live-in partner. Today this is perfectly acceptable in some congregations but difficult in others.

However, it is essential to understand and take into account discordance between a group and a member of that group. Discordance implies a lack of connection between what a group represents and what a member of that group believes and represents.

This means that the knowledge we have about a group will not necessarily be meaningful in an encounter with one member of the group. A member of a Pentecostal congregation or a Muslim community may have completely different views from those represented by the group. We should therefore never think that we know because we have knowledge at the group level, but always *keep an inquiring mind* in encounters with individual clients or families.

EAST MEETS WEST

We can define two main types of culture when comparing Western societies with non-Western societies. *Collectivist* or group-oriented cultures are primarily found in Asia and Africa; here, members prioritize the group above their personal happiness and self-realization. *Individualist* or individual-oriented cultures are primarily found in the USA and Western Europe. A typical feature of an individualist culture is that its members give priority to their own happiness and self-realization above the interests of the group when these interests conflict. "Me" and "my needs and my interests" (perhaps also my children and my family) are the most important factors.

We will now explore the distinctive features of these two extremes and discuss how people can be marked by both cultures at the same time. In family therapy, it is important to understand the communication that can develop in interaction between representatives of these two main types of culture.

COLLECTIVIST CULTURES

Collectivist Cultures
In a collectivist culture, members prioritize the group over their own happiness and self-realization. The family model is the extended family.

Collectivist cultures are found all over the world, but mostly in Asia, Latin America and Africa. Many of the people in the world live in these cultures. Collectivist cultures were also historically the most common type of culture. Today, they are found as an element of all cultures and in all countries. In collectivist cultures, values and norms such as mutual dependence, submission and duty are central aspects. Collectivist cultures are also more or less dominated by a collective understanding of reality.

From an extreme collectivist culture where the individual is more or less absent, we find a gradual progression to an individualistic Western culture. The difference between a collectivist and an individualist culture becomes apparent when the interests of the individual take precedence over the interests of the group. The interests of the individual might then be prioritized over the interests of the family and the needs of the individual might be more important than those of the group.

In Asian and African cultures, traditional family patterns dominate the culture in many contexts. In traditional families, the members are willing to give up many personal ambitions in favour of what is best for the family as a whole. We still see this in many Asian and African cultures, but also in those parts of Western culture that are influenced by Pakistani and other collectivist traditions. When a couple starts a family, it does merely concern the couple themselves, but all the close relatives. "The interests of the individual must be subordinated to those of the group. The group (the family) therefore has a duty to take care of the individual" (Johannessen 2007). It is not uncommon for parents to actively participate in the selection of a spouse. The marriage is arranged by the family, and the future bride or bridegroom is only involved in the choice to a certain extent. In extreme cases, the person is "married off" and is not considered as having the right to choose a spouse. In this way, the family's interests are protected in terms of religion, status and property.

In collectivist cultures, people often live in larger groups than the nuclear family. A young man from Egypt said that he lived in a house in a small town with his parents, aunts, uncles, brothers, sisters and cousins. He thought there were currently 63 or 65 family members living together, but he was not quite sure. As the family grew, they built extensions to their house.

In the year 2000, only 4% of children in the USA lived in households that included three generations. A study of the way of life of middle-class families in Hawaii showed that only 6% of children in white families were looked after by grandparents or aunts and uncles every day, while in Japanese-American families, the figure was 64% (Rogoff 2003).

Collectivist cultures are often hierarchically organized. This could imply, for example, that the oldest man in the extended family has the most authority and that no important decisions can be made without his approval. The family may well consist of three generations and include aunts, uncles, cousins and other relatives. It is thus commonly the oldest man who speaks to others on behalf of the extended family.

When a professional who comes from an individualist culture meets families who belong to a collectivist culture, they will need to take their time to find a way of working together that is satisfactory for both parties. In such situations, the therapist must always take the time to ask relevant questions and listen to the family's suggestions about what is needed to create a satisfactory situation or a useful long-term way of working together. In encounters of this kind, we cannot merely rely on our knowledge of typical features of other cultures, but instead focus on our interaction with this particular individual or family here and now.

INDIVIDUALIST CULTURES

Individualist cultures are primarily found in Europe and the USA. In Western society, the individual's self-realization takes precedence over the interest of the group. In individualist cultures, values such as self-fulfilment, independence and freedom are central. It is important to develop an independent self, an individual identity. The history of the family in Europe illustrates the transition to an individualist culture where the individual family member's career and happiness comes before creating and raising the next generation (Shorter 1979). One example of this is that the individual's independent choices now determine when a new family is started.

> **Individualist Cultures**
> In an individualist culture, members prioritize their own happiness and self-realization above the interests of the group when these conflict. "Me" and "my needs and my interests" (perhaps also my children and my family) take precedence. The family model is the nuclear family.

This can be linked to the rise of romanticism. In three different areas, romanticism has helped to undermine the traditional family (Shorter 1979). Firstly, *love* became a reason for marriage. Secondly, the *mother-child relationship* took on a new importance. In the *traditional* family, a mother was even willing to abandon her child in the struggle to survive. The survival of the family came before the care of the children. In the *modern* family, children have been given priority. Thirdly, the family had to *detach itself from the outside world*. In the traditional period, "the family's shell was pierced full of holes, permitting people from outside to flow freely through the household, observing and monitoring" (Shorter 1977, p. 5). Traffic also went in the opposite direction as family members could feel that they had more in common with peer groups outside the family. The rise of romantic love increased the focus on the individual and the nuclear family was clearly separated from the extended family. The family became an emotional unit rather than a place of production and reproduction.

Hybrid Forms

Certain collectivist ideas have survived in some religious subcultures in the Western world. In some of these, the good of the group is more important than individual betterment. In certain religious groups, the sense of group belonging has been more important than individual freedom in, for example, choosing a wife or husband. Collectivist notions can also be found in working-class cultures where an individual's pursuit of a career or "social climbing" is seen as betraying the group.

The relationship between individual-oriented and group-oriented cultures is thus more complex than it may appear at first glance. The two phenomena can also co-exist both on an individual and cultural level; a person can be assertive and independent at work but family-oriented at home (Jørgensen and van der Weele 2009).

Encounters Between People from Collectivist and Individualist Cultures

In discussing collectivist and individualist cultures, we find it difficult to point to cultures where their typical features are found in pure form. However, we do find some extremes. In a multicultural society, different ideas about the relationship between individual and group will meet and challenge each other.

Globalization affects the ways in which we relate to and understand the relationship between collectivist and individualist cultures. As people move and migrate, all countries will include both types of culture among their population. The past 40 years in Europe have seen a significant increase in collectivist culture through immigration from India, Pakistan, Somalia and other Asian and African countries. There has also been a significant rise in adherents of previously unfamiliar religious groups such as Muslims, Hindus and Buddhists. Interaction between people from collectivist and individualist cultures is therefore taking place here and now, where we all live and work. This provides opportunities to develop new forms of therapeutic practice.

The meeting of collectivist and individualist cultures also presents some difficulties. We can find strongly ethnocentric comments and attitudes from traditional Western culture and from religious and political groups. Such difficulties are particularly likely to arise when certain people "know" what is best, what is right and how we should live. Imposing such attitudes upon others forms a basis for conflict. We see this when representatives of an individualist culture want to impose their family models and ways of organizing family life on other cultures. Similarly, collectivist-oriented people might have a quite different view of Western individual freedom, freedom of expression or individuality in clothes, art and other forms of cultural expression. When curiosity and openness are lost, they may be replaced by authoritarian ideas and actions from the members of both cultures.

Problems can arise when a collectivist way of raising children meets Western individualist forms of upbringing. Different views on what children should be responsible for, how children should behave and how physical discipline is used can create tensions.

RELIGION AND CULTURE

The importance of religion varies greatly between people. However, there has been a tendency to overlook or neglect the significance of religion in our attempts to understand culture and relationships between cultures. The conflicts in the Middle East are telling examples of this. In the Oslo peace process, for example, religious organizations were not invited to participate in the negotiations (Akerhaug 2008). In recent years, however, religion has taken on increased significance in the understanding of conflicts and problems between people and between cultures.

In Western culture, religion is traditionally considered as a private matter. Religion is not usually shared or talked about in public. Neither do people ask about it or have the right to know anything about it when they meet others. However, this is not how people think about religion in all cultures. In Islamic countries such as Saudi Arabia and Iran, for example, there is no clear boundary between politics, society and religion. Religion influences and controls understandings and practices in both politics and society.

Just as we cannot view Islam or Judaism as a homogeneous entity, we find a wide variety of beliefs and practices within Christian culture. If we generalize, we disregard the diversity of reality, which also applies to the field of religion. If we know some things about a certain religion, we may think we have relevant knowledge when we meet individuals who profess that religion, but that may not be meaningful at all.

Many people make efforts to promote dialogue between religions, in schools and in society. "In order to achieve equal dialogue, it is necessary to present different religions and views of life on the basis of their uniqueness and how they understand themselves" (Aasen 2012, p. 111).

In dialogue, we seek *understanding*, not *agreement*. As family therapists who encounter different religions and views of life, we should try to explore the subjective understandings of each individual client. This will promote dialogue, whether the client belongs to a familiar or unfamiliar religion or has a non-religious outlook on life. Dialogue can help us to realize that there exists a diversity of religious and non-religious approaches to existential questions while we still keep to our own religion or point of view.

Cultures and Subcultures

Most cultures consist of subcultures or subgroups of people who belong together. The strength of a subculture will strike the visitor to a "Norwegian" church in Minnesota in the USA. Although it is many generations since most of the families emigrated from Norway, they still have their Norwegian churches and some of these denominations have grown in recent years. In Minneapolis there is a Norwegian memorial church with a Norwegian priest who still sometimes conducts services in Norwegian. This illustrates the strength of religious, social and cultural communities.

A culture such as Norwegian culture consists of a large number of subcultures. Social class, religion, political beliefs, fraternal organizations and ethnicity form the basis of various subcultures. These may be political subcultures, national subcultures, religious subcultures, or subcultures of music, art or fashion. Many people belong to more than one subculture.

The term multicultural can be used to describe those belonging to several cultures, and some people argue for the use of hyphenated words to denote new cultural groups such as Norwegian-Pakistani or Norwegian-Vietnamese.

"Today I would say that I am a human being, a citizen of the world, who is Norwegian, Pakistani, Muslim and a social democrat—and if someone tells me to go back to where I came from, I will go back to Lier [a town in Norway]. What does this tell you about my sense of belonging?" asks the author.

And he answers himself: "It tells you that Norway is and will always be a multicultural society, and nothing can change that" (Zaman 1999, p. 15).

Religious groups that use common dress codes and other symbolic forms of expression, such as Brunstad Christian Church and some Muslim groups, show their religious affiliation by dressing in certain ways or wearing certain hairstyles, such as the pigtails worn by women in Brunstad Christian Church. Another good example of this is the Amish in the USA who still dress, live and travel as people did in the nineteenth century. They live in farming communities and use horses and carts and dress in traditional clothes from the 1800s. They have no electricity and rarely use cars. Forms of expression of religious subcultures can also be more indirect, as in the Laestadians, a religious group mainly found in the Nordic countries who do not watch TV, go to the cinema, drink alcohol, dress up or go dancing. In this way, they stand out from the rest of society and their religious affiliation becomes visible.

Other subcultures only become visible when you meet and talk to members or know the secret signs they use to show who they are. This applies, for example, in Masonic lodges where the members meet and have secret rituals. They also make themselves known to each other when they meet outside the lodge by greeting in a particular way. We must also remember that as family therapists we ourselves represent a subculture within the culture. Further, our professional subculture consists of sub-subcultures.

RELIGIONS IN DIFFERENT CULTURES

Most people in the world belong to a religion. About 80% of the world's population is a member of a major religion. Christianity accounts for 2.3 billion or 33%. Three of the world's main religions have their origins in Asia, namely Islam, Hinduism and Buddhism. About 1.5 billion (25%)

adhere to Islam, while around 1.2 billion (15%) are Hindus and roughly 500 million (7%) are Buddhists.

Within these groups we find considerable differences. In Christianity there are Catholics and various Reformed churches. In Islam, there are Sunni and Shia Muslims, who to some extent view each other as opponents. In addition, there are a number of smaller religious groups such as Jews, Jehovah's Witnesses and (mostly in Africa) various traditional religions.

There are also a number of practices that belong to both religion and secular techniques for physical exercise and contemplation. Examples of these are various forms of meditation and yoga.

SRI YANTRA

One of our students told us that the family had this symbol on the wall at home. It is an important Hindu symbol that reminds us of our interconnection with nature and the divine.

The symbol was an image of the cosmos, with the feminine and masculine integrated.

According to the student, the symbol was used in meditation in the temple or at home and was a reminder of love as the most important force in life.

NON-RELIGIOUS SPIRITUALITY

We wish to avoid a strict definition of spirituality. There is a wide variety of spiritual activities that are not explicitly linked to any specific religious practice. However, as we can see, there is rarely a sharp distinction between religious and non-religious aspects. Many activities cater to a wide variety of people and may include rituals to which participants ascribe different meanings.

Meditation is a form of religious practice originating from Hinduism, Buddhism and Christianity, which in the past 40–50 years has been taken over and developed in a number of secular contexts. These practices also have much in common with prayer. Mindfulness is a widespread form of meditation with roots in Buddhist thinking that many people have practised in secular contexts in recent decades. Mindfulness is often referred to as "attentive presence" and is promoted to help people who suffer from stress and other burdens in life.

A number of fraternal organizations also include significant elements of religious rituals in their local practice to admit new members or promote existing ones to higher levels. Examples of these are the Freemasons and the Odd Fellows.

SIMILARITIES IN FORMS OF COMMUNICATION AND CULTURE

Religious and spiritual practices usually include rituals and fixed forms of behaviour where the practice is manifested by bodily movements. People fold their hands, kneel, make the sign of the cross, walk in processions, hold hands, lie flat, etc. Holy Communion is an example of a ritual that includes the senses of taste and smell. The sense of smell is also involved in the use of incense and flowers. Most rituals can be performed individually or in groups. These are some examples of similar forms of expression used in religious practices.

There is much to suggest that some similar forms of expression are universal and presumably innate. For example, children born deaf-blind smile, laugh and cry in the same way as hearing and sighted children (Jandt 1995). Although it would seem that we find similar forms of expression across cultures, their meaning may still vary from culture to culture.

Praying with the Clients?
The therapist Susie had her last session with a couple. They had been seeing each other regularly for several months, and now the couple was moving. The man in the relationship was a priest, and the couple called themselves Christians. In closing, the man asked if they should say a prayer. Therapist Susie asked if one of them wanted to pray, but they wanted her to. Susie was very doubtful, she had not prayed with clients before. Admittedly she shared their beliefs, but therapists weren't supposed to pray with clients, were they? And what should she pray about in that case? But it was the couple's wish, so after thinking about it, she said a short prayer for God's mercy on the couple and their way forward.

SPIRITUALITY IN DIFFERENT FAMILY CULTURES
AND THE THERAPIST'S OWN SPIRITUALITY

Spirituality is present and visible in varying degrees in different families. Some families would not describe any of their activities as spiritual, while other families would link spirituality to most of their activities. Some families do not participate in any spiritual activities in church, meditation, yoga, singing or music. Further, meditation, yoga, music and singing are not necessarily connected to spirituality. We find a wide variety of forms of spirituality, ranging from a completely passive variety to one that fills a person's whole life.

Members of the same family may relate to spirituality in completely different ways. Some family members may be very active or fond of traditions and keen to maintain them, while others may be quite indifferent to such expressions of spirituality.

Some therapists do not take part in spiritual or religious activities, while others are actively involved. Regardless of the therapist's own relationship to spirituality, he or she must be able to accept clients in their lifeworld and show respect for it. If a therapist meets a family that lives a life that largely mirrors the therapist's own life (such as belonging to the same congregation or meditation group), the therapist risks becoming "home blind", thus not hearing or realizing what the clients are saying. Here, the therapist's cultural sensitivity will be of great importance.

CULTURAL SENSITIVITY

We can acquire knowledge about culture and study different cultures; this will provide us with a form of cultural competence, i.e. sound knowledge of cultural traditions, religions and political systems. This is general knowledge about the group level in a culture. Cultural sensitivity, on the other hand, refers to how sensitive we are in encounters with people from another culture, including our sensitivity to traditions and behaviour in this culture. It also involves awareness of our own life story and our own attitudes and norms (Qureshi 2009). We can also think of cultural sensitivity as a professional approach in encounters with people from other cultures.

Cultural sensitivity is a method that opens questions based on the most significant differences and similarities. One can have an almost infinite number of culturally sensitive questions and each question can lead to even more questions. (Qureshi 2009, p. 270)

In this way, cultural sensitivity can be systematically acquired. If we are aware that every meeting with clients and families can be considered a meeting of cultures, we can attempt to improve our sensitivity and our understanding of encounters with people from other cultures. We can thus develop a cultural competence where the sum of our cultural knowledge and sensitivity is manifested in specific encounters with different people.

THE PROFESSIONAL'S CULTURE MEETS THE CLIENT'S CULTURE

When a professional's culture meets a client's culture, will it help the professional to have detailed knowledge of the culture of the client? Should we read another book and take another course to improve our understanding? Barbara Rogoff (2003) argues that specializing in categorization of cultural subgroups will lead us down the wrong path. Her solution to this problem is to move away from thinking that culture consists of different categories that can be used to describe communication between participants in an interaction context.

We should therefore stop thinking that we are meeting another culture and start thinking in terms of a meeting with another person, from another culture. We know nothing about the person in advance. One meets a person, not a culture. The knowledge that arises in our encounter will form the basis for our contact, rather than all our general cultural knowledge.

Despite this, cultural understanding is a fundamental field to study for family therapists. The need for cultural understanding in professional work is closely linked to the idea of equal treatment for all. This ideal assumes that each individual and each family will receive help based on their own values and culture. Paradoxically, equal treatment presupposes that everyone is treated differently, based on the context and the culture with which they identify. Professionals should be familiar with methods that can provide a more interpretative approach in cultural encounters (Johannessen 2006).

Conflicts will sometimes arise between therapists and families. These may be value conflicts where, for example, women's position in the family and society is far removed from the therapist's values. If deep value conflicts are revealed in the collaboration between therapist and family, dialogue will be needed to enhance the therapist's reflexivity.

By making efforts to understand families' spirituality, professionals can clarify their own values and norms and the relationship between their values and their professional duties and loyalties. Dialogue can help us to clarify how cultural differences, family differences, or issues of gender, age, religion, and class affect the collaboration. This can be a useful framework for understanding the problems to be solved together.

As a young family therapist, I went on a home visit to a single mother with 3 small children. Life was difficult for her, she had trauma both from her childhood and the life with her divorced husband. The woman was Muslim, from a country in North Africa. She was depressed and used the word "Inshallah", in almost every sentence. I knew that this word meant "if God wants", but I did not know how to use this in my contact with her. I thought it was better to leave it alone. (Åse)

SPIRITUAL-CULTURAL DIFFERENCES IN COUPLE'S AND FAMILY RELATIONSHIPS

Today, interfaith marriage is very common. People travel the world, and there is great tolerance for choosing one's own faith. Even if couples basically have the same religion or outlook on life, cultural differences can still be large. An example could be a Christian couple, where one is what we can call conservative, and is concerned with interpreting the Bible literally. The other is perhaps liberal and wants to interpret the Bible metaphorically and link it to our time. Since the spiritual framework is deep and vulnerable in man, this can lead to distance and major conflicts. If the couple is exposed to stress or various stresses, their tolerance for each other may decrease. Challenges can also arise when the couple have children, linked to spiritual guidance and religious traditions.

The generation above can also make an impression. One woman said that when their children were small, the husband, who was an atheist, did not want to baptize the children. The woman was a Christian, and although the children were now of primary school age, this was something that lay like a veil over the relationship, and she had difficulty accepting this. This helped to create an emotional distance, and they struggled with a way to deal with this. When the crises come, it might be difficult to share the spiritual life, as they are at different points of view.

Here, therapists might be of great help by improving communication, exploring differences, and developing mutual respect and compassion and identifying spiritual resources. It will be important to explore what makes sense for the individual. Here it would be wise to tread carefully and not push your own beliefs or philosophy of life on the clients. We should have a multifaith perspective and help family members to find meaning, connection on the life journey (Walsh 2010).

Reflections

---

1. Look at the figure below:
   • What are the stories behind your spiritual life?
   • What kind of tradition and culture have you been a part of?

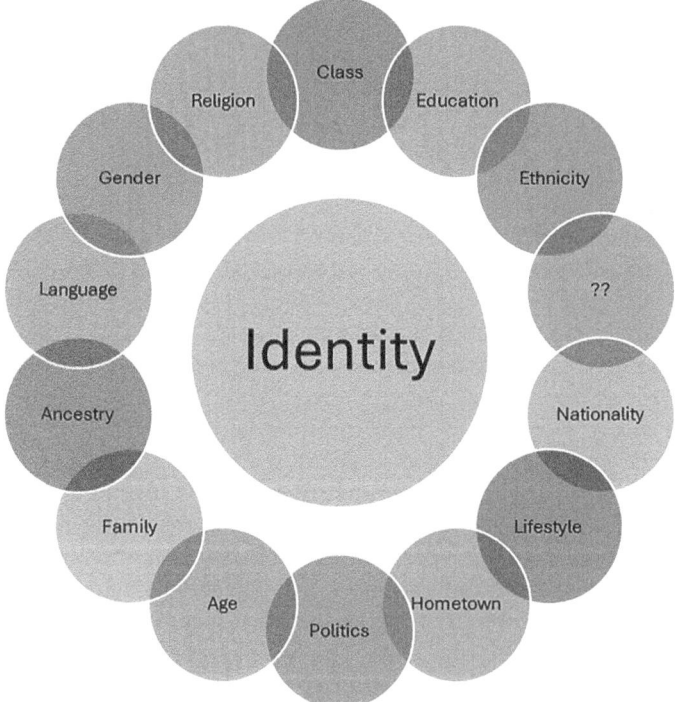

2. What was important to you before, but not important now? What is important to you now that was not important before?
3. Which people have been decisive for you in your spiritual development?

REFERENCES

Akerhaug, L. (2008). *Jøder—ikke bare jøder.* Forskning.no.

Eriksen, T. H. (2021). *Små steder - store spørsmål: innføring i sosialantropologi* (4. utgave. ed.). Universitetsforlaget.

Jandt, F. E. (1995). *Intercultural communication: an introduction.* Sage.

Johannessen, E. (2007). *Mye er forskjellig - men bare utenpå?: om barn, barneoppdragelse og utdanning i en mangfoldig verden.* Sebu forl.

Johannessen, Ø. L. (2006). Coping with cultural encounters in education. In (pp. s. 171–183). Unipub forl./Oslo Academic Press.

Jørgensen, H., & van der Weele, J. (2009). Vold i storfamiliekontekst–erfaringer fra Alternativ til Vold. *Eide, NA Qureshi, M. Rugkåsa & H. Vike (Red.), Over profesjonelle barrierer. Et minoritetsperspektiv i psykososialt arbeid med barn og unge.* Oslo: Gyldendal Akademisk.

Qureshi, N. A. (2009). Kultursensitivitet i profesjonell yrkesutøvelse. In (pp. 206–230). Gyldendal akademisk.

Rogoff, B. (2003). *The cultural nature of human development* (1st ed.). Oxford University Press.

Shorter, E. (1977). *The making of the modern family.* Fontana.

Shorter, E. (1979). *Kernefamiliens historie.* Nyt nordisk forlag.

Vike, H., & Eide, K. (2009). Kulturanalyse, minoritetsperspektiv og psykososialt arbeid. In (pp. s. 13–37). Gyldendal akademisk.

Walsh, F. (2010). Spiritual Diversity: Multifaith Perspectives in Family Therapy [Article]. *Family Process, 49*(3), 330–348. https://doi.org/10.1111/j.1545-5300.2010.01326.x

Zaman, K. (1999). *Norge i svart, hvitt og brunt: en multikulturell mosaikk.* Forum Aschehoug.

Aasen, J. (2012). *Flerkulturell pedagogikk: en innføring* (Rev. utg. ed.). Oplandske bokforl.

CHAPTER 5

Obstacles to Including Spirituality in Therapy

I believe the best criticism of the bad, is the practice of the better.
—*Richard Rohr*

THE BIG SILENCE

As we already have written, until recently, spirituality was regarded as "out of bounds" in most psychotherapeutic work. Neither was it discussed in textbooks, journals and conferences. For us this has created uncertainty about how to "do spirituality" in practice, and also a lack of competence. Paradoxically, client participation is important in the field, as is meaning-making in co-creation in a systemic/ecological perspective, but despite this, spirituality has been definitely "out". As Gergen (2009) says: "Personal values, spiritual insights, commitments to other traditions - are largely discounted" (p. 27). This was also our informants' experience. They found many obstacles to including clients' spiritual lives. But what were these obstacles? We will now share some stories from therapists and clients from our study. All quotes are from the thesis, and all the informants have been given fictitious names (Holmberg 2018).

Therapists' Experiences

How Do You Name "It"?

Considering the situation for private people's spiritual lives in our part of the world, it is no wonder we have little idea about how to put the topic into words. Spirituality is a multifaceted term, and many therapists find the word "spiritual" difficult to use. Thor, for example, thought that spirituality was an academic word and felt that it was better to ask clients what is important in life, what principles they have in life and what they believe in. At the same time, he recognized that he did not have a relationship with spiritual matters himself, and he never asked about a client's religious life, or the client's relationship to something greater than us or something divine.

For Edwin, spirituality was a strange word, and he used words like values, the purpose of life, meaning and life philosophy. He said that his work could help clients to rediscover dignity, hope, love and meaning and that this could give them a spiritual experience. He added that even though he no longer professed a particular religion, he still often experienced a divine presence in what he called "a healing moment".

Magnus presented himself as Christian, but did not like the words spiritual and religion. He found both concepts indefinable and distant. He used the word faith. He felt that talking about clients' spiritual lives needed to be practically oriented, connected to everyday life. People's faith affects other perspectives in life.

Not Accepted in the Family Therapy Culture

All the therapists who took part in this study felt that spirituality was an under-communicated topic, with no obvious place in Western family therapy culture. It was not an element of serious therapeutic work. It was not a theme where therapists should stay within its parameters. Most therapists therefore do not talk to their colleagues about this topic and are unsure of what their colleagues think about it. When, in addition, it is not discussed either in literature or at conferences, this creates a feeling that it is politically incorrect. Some of the therapists also believed that the methods used in the field make it difficult to bring in spiritual perspectives. When clients bring their problems, a broad framework for life is rarely discussed.

In the 60s, when Tomas started working, he saw how social workers and psychologists were radicalized, and a revolt against the authorities arose. He found that religion and Christianity were perceived as a form of oppression, which they were, in his opinion. He felt that the revolt was necessary but also that it was more about criticism of religious practice and dogma than faith itself. He also believed that the old conflict between the religious and the material was one reason why spirituality had become an under-communicated topic.

Magnus said that his workplace in mental health had a reductionist view of humanity and was negative to spirituality. He believed that this had made him cautious, but also uncertain. If the topic is to come up, he needs the client to specifically ask for it. He thought that most clients do not expect to include this dimension of human life in a psychiatric context. This was also supported by Siri and Kari, who had never talked about spiritual matters with their clients. This was despite the fact that they worked with Christian therapists, who also never included the topic. They knew that their colleagues were Christians, because they had talked about it in private settings. Kari found it rather strange that the therapists talked about morning prayers and Bible texts in private, but never professionally.

In our study, in addition to individual interviews, we included a group of therapists (from Norway), for whom spirituality is very important. They told us why they close the door on the spiritual in professional contexts:

> *Usually, when we come up with such an interpretation, we are seen as a bit exotic, but sometimes also perhaps that we're not quite normal. And some people think this is just nonsense, and especially, many people think it is unprofessional. So in the same way as the clients. … when they enter the therapy room, they do not start by presenting a certain type of spiritual thinking. They test the therapist by coming up with keywords, and … and if the therapist hangs on, then they can continue. And of course, we do the same as … professionals, we quickly realize when … professionals, therapists either shake their heads or roll their eyes or somehow show that this is so uninteresting and unprofessional. "Let's get down to business!" Then we stop talking about it … We react in the same way as the clients do.*

Reflections of Colleagues
Siri said she just followed the practice at her workplace. If spirituality was normally part of the work, she would probably include it, but for now it

was just in her mind during the sessions. "Now no one talks about it, and then it does not exist". The therapy group described how difficult it was to cooperate with other therapists who think that including spirituality is unprofessional. Often, they closed the door:

> *I cannot present something to a person who doesn't know what I'm talking about. I also think clients think in that way too. In the same way, as a therapist, I don't want to present something to a colleague that I immediately can see won't understand it. Then I'd stop doing it at once.*

Several of the therapists said that the people they worked with were of crucial importance. If they felt that they had a lot in common with the other therapists, it was easier to go into the client's spiritual world in therapy.

Excluded from Family Therapy Education

Most of the therapists had no experience of any inclusion of spirituality in their education. This made it a non-topic. Siri said she had no experience or training about how to incorporate the topic and therefore had no thoughts about its usefulness. Her experience was that spirituality was reduced to psychology. That made it difficult to find motivation or direction.

Magnus said that "major life stories" were left out of the family therapy course. He found it difficult to talk about his Christian faith in class. He had to choose his words carefully. Based on his faith, he was sure that God had guided him to the family therapy course and helped him through it, but explained that it would not be a good idea to talk about that: "You're seen as an idiot. … I'm in the middle of my life, relatively well educated and I should have the 'backbone' to choose my own words, but I haven't".

A Secular Society

Nina said that we live in a secular society that affects us all. She felt that this societal discourse was pervading people's lives. Religion and the soul were not part of the conversation. She believed that people were afraid to have an opinion about something, afraid of being categorized, afraid of offending someone. Being neutral and accepting everything had become an important value. This also involved religious neutrality. Nina felt that this eliminated people's feelings and contact with their values.

Kari found it easier to talk about values and meaning than religion and faith. Because of the discourse in society, which includes the split between science and religion, she felt that clients had the idea that the world of psychology was sceptical about religion.

More Critical of Christianity

Several therapists said that even though Christianity is Norway's main religion, it seemed to be less frequently encountered than other religions. Frode had found that several Christian clients had tried to explore his relationship to religion before coming to him for therapy. They had been afraid of not being taken seriously in the public health system. Frode felt that believing was important, and sometimes necessary for recovery. He said:

> *The question is whether it is professional to write off this mindset as 'magical thinking', irrelevant to treatment. I think to ignore certain forms of faith is not professional. It shows a lack of interest and respect for the individual universe, a universe of pain but also opportunities.*

Frode's impression today was that any form of Christianity is often rejected, while Buddhism was embraced and formed part of acceptable psychology. Magnus and Grete had similar experiences. Magnus said that talking about mindfulness, yoga and qigong is ok, but Christian faith is not ok. He wondered what this was all about, since Christianity is the main religion in Norway. Grete found it much easier to talk with Muslim clients about their faith than with Christians. For Muslims, she explained, it is a language, their whole existence, they are more open. If she encountered resistance from Christian clients, it was easier to discontinue the topic and just close that space.

Lacking Language

Many of the therapists had many personal obstacles and said that they lacked language to talk about spirituality; it might be embarrassing, too personal, not relevant to the subject at hand, or they were afraid of getting involved in the client's religious life.

Siri, who had been both Christian and Muslim, said she had no interest in including spirituality in her practice. She had no experience with it, no knowledge and no habit of even talking about it, so she has no motivation to take the theme seriously. She did not know why and how and felt that if clients were concerned about it they would probably bring it up themselves.

Niels, a theologian and former priest, felt untrained and said he had no good tools. He felt unsure of how to relate to a spiritual client, it was like a "scary black hole". How much would he say about his own faith? He was afraid his background would have a negative effect on the therapeutic dialogue.

Several of the therapists found it difficult to talk to clients whose problems felt close to their own spiritual or religious struggles. Tomas, for example, said that some clients have traumatic experiences from belonging to a church in their younger years, and because of his own experiences, he sometimes found it difficult to get involved in their conflicts. He could clearly see how he sometimes avoided questions and moved on to another theme. Ada, who was born in a Muslim country, could also identify with this. She did not want to be associated with Islam, which made her more careful, holding spiritual perspectives back. She did not want clients to think that these matters were important to her. Grete said that the topic felt too private and sensitive and it also created some emotions in her own life. She did not really know why she felt uncomfortable but was afraid the conversation would be unnatural, difficult or strange.

Terje, who mostly provided couples therapy, never asked clients about their worldview. He said that it did not fit in the methodological approach of his workplace and was outside its mandate. On the one hand, he believed that spirituality was taboo, while on the other, his workplace was more concerned with the practical issues of improving contact between couples. Terje said that they used short interventions, where there was limited time to go into broader life questions. He also mentioned the risk of being normative when talking about spirituality. To include God in therapy was out of the question. That was a job for a priest or maybe a psychologist.

CLIENTS' EXPERIENCES

We will now move on to clients' experiences and reflections. Learning from clients can be the best way to develop our practice.

Experiences of a Dualistic Practice

Several of the clients said that family therapy was often practically oriented and lacking in spiritual perspectives. Bjørn found this a problem, as people's spirituality affected relationships, crises and conflicts. People cannot cut their beliefs out of their relationships: "You do not live in a vacuum in relation to your faith". Maja had similar reflections:

> *I am a whole person; all my parts are one. The spiritual part and the bodily part affect each other. … My mind, what I'm doing and reading, what I'm eating. I think everything sort of blends together, I think in a very holistic way. It is impossible to avoid the part of the brain that has to do with the big questions. If you do not include reflections on values, then the therapy will fail. You know, on the top of the cake, there's the icing. Underneath, you find the "big" questions.*

Tuva was raised in a fundamentalist family and learned to keep away from public health care. It took many years before she dared to approach the public health service, and now she found it very important to include all aspects of being human. She said:

> *Since I grew up with some sort of barrier against it, it was really scary, but now it's important for me to glue these pieces together. And to be able to present the "whole me" is important. I don't want to go somewhere with one part and another place with a second part. I think that is important.*

Necessary Obstacles

The clients described spirituality as a vulnerable topic and said that it was sometimes necessary to leave it out. Bjørn said that there can be huge differences in a couple, and if they are not in tune or have problems listening to each other, it is better to put the topic aside. There must be an interest from both sides to go into it.

Tone and Lisbeth had both experienced a violent husband and felt that when there is an imbalance of power, it is wise to leave the topic alone. Lisbeth said:

> *That was my experience. She* [the therapist] *left it out. … I remember he* [her ex-husband] *talked about God, how spiritual he was, and how terrible I was in the eyes of God, but it was just left out. … And this is very important, it would just be another thing to be attacked about.*

Neither of the women could be honest about their spiritual life with their ex-husbands.

Waiting for the Therapist to Include the Topic

Although many clients wanted to incorporate spirituality into the practice, this did not mean that they wanted to introduce it themselves. As John put it: "You don't cross the boundary, you don't force open the door; you wait to be invited".

The clients were unsure whether it was appropriate and would like therapists to be more active. This also applied to differences in the couple's relationship and the family as a whole. Henrik said that therapy can be a place where family members can listen to each other, help respect and tolerance to grow, and also reflect on the spiritual differences that affect the family. This was supported by Maja, who had the following reflection:

> *We have a lot of experience of therapy, which is continuing. It's obvious that we have greatly benefited from therapy, but it could have given us much more if the therapist was more proactive in questioning, wondering and insisting on exploring the differences between us, especially when it comes to our spiritual needs.*

Maja's experiences of therapy over the years were that therapy sessions are often haphazard: just come and talk. She was tired of superficial conversations. She had found that all therapists were waiting for the client's input, and then repeated what they said. Once she tried to raise the question of spiritual needs in a session. Her husband replied that he did not agree, and the therapist did not follow it up. The dialogue came to nothing. "The problem is just that they do not follow up … next time. So one thing is to listen once, then you are only on the surface again of a new series of thoughts and feelings". After many years of therapy, she felt resigned. She did not feel that spiritual aspects of human life were accepted.

A Therapist's Competence and Experience Are Important

Bjørn said that for him it was crucial that the therapist could ask some relevant questions. He could sense whether the therapist felt comfortable talking about it or not. If the therapist felt uncomfortable, it was very easy to close the door.

For Tone, the crucial factor had been to have a therapist who had an understanding of the topic and had "inside information" about it. She said that with her current therapist, she could even joke about the church, even though it was very important to her. She would never have done that if the therapist knew nothing about church life. She did not want to speak ill of the church. Tuva had had similar experiences:

It makes it very easy to talk about. I don't need to say much before he understands it, and he can very easily provide relevant feedback. It makes it much easier. If I had met someone who was very religious, part of some congregation, I maybe would have felt it was a bit frightening, and maybe thought we could just put this part of me away and maybe just talk about other things.

A sense of security seemed to be important. Meeting a therapist with knowledge and experience, who included the topic in an appropriate manner.

Tone said that she had previously been married to a man who abused her psychologically and sexually. She had grown up in a pastor's family, and she felt guilty for wanting to divorce her husband. In addition, the man was a leader in the church they belonged to. There he seemed kind, spiritual and extroverted, and she had no one to talk to there. She desperately needed someone to talk to about her frustrations but was very surprised when she realized that the therapist had no idea how this could play out in this context:

The therapist did not understand. He said, "So what?" For me, it was very strange, and I felt that he couldn't understand my Christian background, that even such a cruel man is hard to leave because it's wrong in a way. ... And I felt it was something about our connection, because this "room" was so big in my life, and with the therapist, I needed to close the door. I could talk about everything else, there were thousands of things, but I felt it wasn't fruitful to continue. ... I just felt that a door was closed, you know; he didn't understand me at all. I felt I was a problem.

She wanted the therapist to look into her situation, just listen and reflect and wonder together with her. What kind of reactions would make her suffer if she got divorced and maybe God was angry at her? She did not know how to deal with it, but understood that she could not continue with the therapist:

I go very quiet when someone does not understand me, sitting there with my questions. No, there's no point in talking about it. It just becomes a non-issue. So, the only thing I did [in response] *was to quit, you see. I realized there was no point in continuing.*

She had to close a door to a room it was impossible to close.

The Desire for a Transparent Therapist

Several of the clients said that they would like to know something about the spirituality of the therapists. They felt unsure if therapists could handle talking about spiritual issues. John said: "This is about a lack of language, you're afraid of mentioning, talking about and using spirituality because you don't want to make people embarrassed".

It can create a sense of mutual trust if therapists can understand the strength of a spiritual life, and they must be open and able to respect different kinds of worldviews. In fact, some of the clients wanted to change therapists if their current therapist did not fit in with their spiritual life. On the other hand, Tone said that if therapists feel the topic is too difficult, then they should know other therapists better suited to the client. She compared this to doctors, who refer patients when more expertise is needed:

If a therapist feels spiritual issues are difficult to talk about, I think it's better if the therapist suggests another therapist, because they know someone else who can handle it well. If a doctor didn't know enough about joints, he'd recommend an orthopaedic surgeon.

Tone said that for her God filters into everything, and it would be very difficult to work with a therapist who is an atheist. She needed therapists who have relevant questions and encourage her to talk about all facets of life. This was supported by Lisa, Bjørn and Anette, and Lisa said she would not mention her faith if she did not know the therapist's standpoint. This is a question of resonance. Anette said:

For me and many others, faith is the most important thing, so if it [the therapy] *clashes with your main ideas, then the therapy will kind of fall flat. If you get a match* [with the therapist], *it will be much more solid.*

Bjørn said that if spirituality was raised in a therapy session, he would need to know something about the therapist's spiritual life. He felt that the therapist had to be able to give him something. A common frame of reference would make him feel relaxed and confident.

Religion Seems Difficult for Therapists

Some clients felt that religiosity was a disturbing element. Eva and John had been in couples therapy several times, but never talked about their religious life. Values, yes, but they never linked the values to their religious life. They said they had very different religious backgrounds, and needed to reflect on this. Their beliefs were linked to their values and affected family life, child-rearing and their meaning-making in different ways.

Henrik had similar reflections, saying that God and religion would have been of great help to him but were left out in therapy. They did not fit in with the idea of what professional therapeutic work was "supposed to be", and he thought therapists were afraid of what colleagues would think of them if they went into the topic. The more power you get, the less spirituality. He thought that if therapists expressed religious or spiritual ideas, in the worst cases they would be frozen out.

Anette said that therapists are not allowed to talk about religion. It is not part of their professional work; it is a different dimension. If she had religious problems, she would never think family therapy could help her:

> I don't know what kind of worldview the therapists have. Because of my experience in psychiatry, I'm not sure how Christian beliefs would be perceived and accepted. In some contexts, they are not seen as a resource or something positive.

This was supported by Maja, who spoke about how she and her husband were brought up in Christian traditions and their differences had been difficult for their marriage. They had been in therapy several times over nearly three decades, but never a single word about faith. She felt a bit resigned:

> I believe it really is about time. I've been ready for years. I think it's completely strange those questions haven't arisen before, not a single question for 27 years: What does your faith mean to you in this context?

She added that therapists want to be neutral even if it is an impossible position. She also thought that therapists felt embarrassed when talking about religion. Religion was too private, too private for therapists, in her opinion.

A CRITICAL VIEW OF THE FAMILY THERAPY FIELD

When systems theory was included in psychotherapeutic practice, it had such a great impact that it has been described as a paradigm shift. A very important shift, which for us today feels completely natural and right. However, those who first came up with these ideas were children of their time and part of their own history and tradition. But, interestingly, despite an ecological systemic focus, spiritual perspectives were not presented as part of the whole. Despite the focus on multiple realities (Burr 2015) and Bateson's encouragement to look beyond and contemplate the "pattern" that connects (Bateson 1979), spiritual and religious perspectives have been left out.

Bateson, who was one of the major contributors to communication theory, found it important to see both mind and body as necessary elements. However, he seemed to be more interested in the sacred and spiritual in his final years (Bateson and Bateson 1987). Telfener (2017) says that this holistic thinking is a way of seeing and acting, recognizing the whole, and recognizing the complex.

If we continue in the universe of Bateson, he believed that we could never fully understand the world, we could only have maps of reality (Bateson 1979). To read maps, we need some basic knowledge. We also need to ask ourselves if the map we have is good enough. Has it been updated recently? We need a map which we can call literacy, which includes spiritual, existential and religious perspectives. Human spirituality is there, even if we do not immediately notice it. We all need to look at our maps and explore what place spirituality has in this context. We need critical literacy, which can evaluate our practice, and we need to critically reflect on marginal voices, dominant ideologies and discourses (Luke 2012).

Based on the voices from our study, there is a need for a new and more holistic systemic practice, which also includes people's spiritual life. There has been a culture of silence for years, and it needs to end. We all have a responsibility to critically reflect on our practice, and our professional landscape, and also try to free ourselves from oppressive habits and roles (Freire 1979). The absence of spirituality in practice is also part of our culture and must therefore be raised in the public debate (Honneth 1995). Recognizing and legitimizing this topic, through education, guidance and various oral and written contributions, will help the therapist to work with the topic both personally and professionally. What are the obstacles, or what are the possibilities? Aponte (2009) says, "All therapy rests on a spiritual platform of values and a philosophical outlook that reflects the spirituality of clients and the clinician's therapeutic philosophy" (p. 130). However, a stronger focus on the spiritual will make the therapist more aware of the topic and how to integrate it appropriately. Therapists are not value-neutral or value-free. Value-free practice does not exist. Systemic practice, which is initially not reductionist, becomes reductionist when human perspectives are not taken into account. This is of course serious, but also old-fashioned, and not appropriate for a practice of today. We need a much more reflective approach to this topic. We have to look at patterns that connect in a holistic work for change. As Lisbeth, a client, said:

I am an entire human being; all my parts are one. The spiritual part and the bodily part work on each other, the mind, what I do, what I read, what I eat; everything is involved with my body and my mind in one way or another.

Lisbeth wanted her whole self and her whole life to be recognized.

Reflections

1. Do you have the ability to create a spiritually safe and affirming therapeutic environment for your clients?
2. Do you have the ability and expertise to explore clients' spiritual and religious lives?
3. Can you include clients' spiritual or religious beliefs as part of treatment and healing processes?
4. What do you do if you find that clients' spiritual lives make them get stuck emotionally?
5. Do you know where to seek guidance if you get stuck in such matters?

REFERENCES

Aponte, H. J. (2009). The stress of povertry and the comfort of spirituality. In F. Walsh (Ed.), *Spiritual resources in family therapy* (2 ed., pp. 125–140). The Guliford Press.
Bateson, G. (1979). *Mind and nature: a necessary unity*. Wildwood House.

Bateson, G., & Bateson, M. C. (1987). *Angels fear: towards an epistemology of the sacred*. Macmillan.

Burr, V. (2015). *Social constructionism*. Routledge.

Freire, P. (1979). *Pedagogy of the oppressed*. Sheed and Ward.

Gergen, K. J. (2009). *An invitation to social construction* (2nd ed.). SAGE.

Holmberg, Å. (2018). *Making room for spirituality?: family therapists' and clients' perceptions and experiences about spirituality in family therapy* VID Specialized University]. Oslo.

Honneth, A. (1995). *The struggle for recognition: the moral grammar of social conflicts*. Polity Press.

Luke, A. (2012). Critical literacy: Foundational notes. *Theory into practice*, *51*(1), 4–11.

Telfener, U. (2017). Becoming through Belonging: The Spiritual Dimension in Psychotherapy. *Australian and New Zealand Journal of Family Therapy*, *38*(1), 156–167. https://doi.org/10.1002/anzf.1199

PART II

Practice and Competence

CHAPTER 6

Making Room for Spirituality

> The planet does not need more successful people. The planet
> desperately needs more peacemakers, healers, restorers, storytellers
> and lovers of all kinds.
> —*David W. Orr*

In Part II of this book, we will explore how we as therapists can develop our spirituality and become more open and curious in dealing with clients' spiritual lives. We want to open up the word spirituality and see which perspectives can be accommodated there. We present some perspectives here that we believe are important for a spiritual life. Hopefully this will give you some reflections on your own life, which in turn will make you more open to the spiritual life of your clients. Through these reflections, you may also be able to find a language that can provide a way into the clients' spiritual journey.

Your Spiritual Journey

There are a great many books, articles and courses that offer spiritual development. Many people are rootless and yearn for a deeper connection in life. Spiritual and religious leaders offer higher wisdom and peace of mind. However, it can still be difficult to find a path that provides hope,

© The Author(s), under exclusive license to Springer Nature   99
Switzerland AG 2024
Å. Holmberg, P. Jensen, *Working with Spirituality in Family
Systemic Practice*, Palgrave Texts in Counselling and Psychotherapy,
https://doi.org/10.1007/978-3-031-77310-5_6

faith, healing and blessings for oneself, one's relationships and the world at large. The world needs love and peace like never before. It seems people never learn. Everyone has to find a way that can help to make the world a better place. In a holistic perspective, spirituality is part of human beings, but spiritual awareness will vary throughout our lives. It depends on what we have grown up with, what experiences we have encountered in life and whether we feel a spiritual longing. Our spiritual journey through life can have various stops and take unexpected turns.

As systemic therapists, we meet clients with different kinds of life ideologies and faiths. If we have a natural relationship with our own and others' spiritual lives, it helps us to be more open to what clients have in their hearts.

The power of life has many names. It can be the soul, God, Christ, Allah, the divine, the Universe, the Ultimate or the sacred. Spirituality brings us in touch with the eternal nature of life, a wisdom that guides us on our path. For the authors of this book, this is a universal love that we call God. We believe this love is the creator of everything and influences every human being. The Creator's love and presence are grounded in the created world. As we see it, a spiritual journey starts with the realization that there is a loving force that wants the best for us and wants us to share this force in the world. In this way, there is no distinction between the holy and the profane. The word *uni-verse* refers to the fact that we must stand together as people and take care of the creation on which we are completely dependent. We believe how we act is much more important than having the right doctrine. We think the Franciscan priest Richard Rohr has an important point when he says a loving God in everything and everyone is a key to mental, existential or spiritual health and a kind of basic contentment and happiness. He thinks the more we can move beyond our small ego, the more we can transcend (Rohr 2019).

We are aware that people nourish their spiritual life in different ways. There is no conclusive answer. Nevertheless, we will offer some perspectives here, which we believe may be important. Hopefully, this will help you to find what resonates with you and your life. Perhaps you also have other sources that are not mentioned here.

Giving Less Space to the Ego

Change is difficult. We are in many ways like animals; we like habits and routines. Life goes on, as it always has. We live in a culture where there is a great focus on boosting our ego and thinking about ourselves. However, we believe our ego can block a healthy spirituality, and our self-absorption can become an obstacle to finding inner peace and meeting the other in love.

Ego is not a "thing", but we can use it metaphorically. It is a way to reflect on our lives. Richard Rohr says the ego is that part of the self that wants to be significant, central and important by itself, while others are given less importance. The ego loves the status quo, even if it fails us. He says it can give a sense of security and superiority and prevents us from contacting our soul and our inner life (Rohr 2011). However, we *need* an ego to function as human beings. The ego helps us to function in society by organizing and transforming experiences, and helping us with judgement, impulse control, morality and much more. The problem arises when we become too egocentric and dualistic and lack an ecological understanding. The Canadian psychologist David Benner (2016) says it is like looking at ourselves in the mirror. It tells us something about our inner landscape. We get angry and need to judge and criticize. Benner says that this dualistic judgemental attitude is typical of many people today. He explains:

> *The egoistic self is simply a way of being when we are cut off from the flow of life pulling us toward an alternative organization of self that already exists within us. In so many ways, the alternative way of being is deeper and truer to our humanity. It is more organic, more integral, and more life-enhancing. It is a way of being that places us firmly within the flow of human becoming. It is the way of the heart.* (Benner 2016, p. 83)

Having an awareness of this can help us to have a different focus. Maybe the first step is to think less about ourselves and have a broader focus. Instead of spending a lot of time on social media, we can use the time to find out what nourishes our soul, and do what fills us with love and peace. It is very easy to be influenced by market forces, but maybe we can learn to live with less, and not chase after more and more in a hamster wheel going faster and faster. Is it possible to choose a path that brings hope, peace and reconciliation—and let that shape us when we meet our clients? Our inner life will affect the therapy session. Who we are, our values and our focus in life all matter.

Changing our habits can be difficult. But just like in sport, we need to practice.

Grateful Living
Brother David Steindl-Rast is a 98-year-old author, scholar and Benedictine monk. He is known for his message about gratefulness as the true source of lasting happiness. He has been a source of inspiration and spiritual friendship to many leaders and luminaries worldwide and is an important figure in the modern interfaith dialogue movement.
Look at his little movie about gratefulness, and spend a few minutes afterwards to reflect on what comes to your mind:
https://www.youtube.com/watch?v=3Zl9puhwiyw
SOURCE: https://grateful.org/brother-david/

Being Aware of the Therapist's Power

As therapists, we are in a position of power. Even if we define ourselves as equals in a therapy system, we are still responsible for leading the process and using our expertise to help those who have wanted to come to therapy. When topics are introduced, we have the opportunity to dive deeper, or even to close the topic, if something feels unpleasant for us. If we have a strained relationship with spirituality, including religion, or do not quite know what it is all about, it is easy to ignore it, and not understand how important it can be to people.

On the other hand, if spirituality or religion is very important to us, we must be careful not to impose our views on clients. We believe it is important to recognize that there is not just *one* truth, and we must listen for what gives meaning and life-giving perspectives to the individual client. We also know that this can vary within the individual family, and it is then important to explore the perspectives of the various family members and how they influence each other. However, regardless of their clients' beliefs, family therapists have an ethical and legal responsibility in relation to family relationships to promote kindness and respect and to counteract abuse and oppression.

As human beings and therapists, we are on a journey of lifelong learning, our knowledge is not unchangeable, the complete and absolute truth. We believe we need to be humble, and not force others to adopt our views through our authority. Love has to be our highest goal. By being in touch with our spirituality, we can more easily help clients to find creative and peaceful ways to prevent or end conflicts and to promote and strengthen peace (McLaren 2016).

A Teaching Situation:
A few years ago, I (Åse) taught spirituality for a master's class in mental health care. We had come to a practical task with the question; What is spirituality for you? Åse encouraged the students to be creative; she had brought postcards and drawing materials. Music, pictures, sacred texts, stories and poems could also be useful. The students then shared their stories through various forms, and it became a powerful situation, which evoked emotions in different denominations. I had goosebumps for a long time afterwards thinking about it.

One of the students was very critical of faith and the church, but when it was his turn, he chose to share a poem.

(From Johan Griep, translated into English)

TO BE PICKED UP
Child
has its own way
to use the language.
In the kindergarten there
my son goes
they are, for example, "picked up".
Sunniva, you are picked up!
They are shouting
when for example
Sunniva
is picked up, and Sunniva
drops what she has
in the hands
running squealing
down the slope
right into the arms of the one standing at the gate
and have come to pick her up.
When I, too, once, noticed someone
standing at the gate
and will pick me up
I hope
that it will happen
exactly like that

BRING BACK THE SOUL

Initially, the word psychology was formed by combining the Greek *psychē* (meaning "breath, principle of life, life, soul") with *-logia* (which comes from the Greek *logos*, meaning "speech, word, reason"), and it was defined as "knowledge of the soul". Today, psychology is concerned with the science or study of the mind and behaviour, and the soul seems to be packed away somewhere. Today it seems like most people in the Western world live in a "constructed" world full of technology, stress and a long to-do list, often well away from what nourishes the soul. Many live separated from themselves and have little contact with nature. This creates alienation of living things, even ourselves. For a long time, we have lived in an individualistic, egocentric culture where we strive to be good enough and live up to collective standards. However, human beings are intelligent and try to develop the world for the better. We have seen and benefitted from wonderful inventions, yet we seem to have lost something: contact with our soul. Perhaps it is time to give the soul new space and explore what that might entail.

What is soul? The soul has always been intangible. Some years ago, a doctor conducted a research study on dying people. He weighed them just before the moment of death, and just after death had occurred. The dead people weighed 21.7 grams less. The doctor's conclusion was then that the soul must weigh 21.7 grams (Roach 2003). However, this research has been called fabrication, because where in the body is the soul? And yet it is supposed to be the soul that gives life to a human being. As we see it, the soul gives us a personality; the soul is the actual human being.

Bill Plotkin (2003) believes that the soul is the ultimate meaning. The soul is for everyone, not only religious sub-groups. Contact with our soul makes us feel that we belong to the world. If we know that we will protect, respect and love the world. Plotkin says soul is translated in the Hebrew Bible texts as *nephesh* and has at least eight meanings: life self, a person, longing, desire, hunger and feeling.

Linell Corbett (2011), a professor of depth psychology from California, believes that the soul is the realm of meaning when we look into ourselves. This is when we are inspired or affected by music, art, a ritual, a person, the natural world or duty or love. The soul is what matters to us. The soul is not a thing that can be measured and weighed or an essence within us. The soul is in a way transcendent, reminding us that we are more than biological machines. The soul is the ultimate meaning which is held within us. The soul is inside every living thing and tells it what it is and what it can become. This is deeper than your education, your job or your parenthood. There is something bigger than our ego and universal holiness.

Marilynne Robinson, an American author and literary scholar, is interested in deep humanism and believes that the concept of soul is what most deeply binds us together, an unshakeable foundation for compassion, recognition and love. When we recognize our soul, we will be able to love enemies and welcome strangers. Robinson is critical of determinism and reductionism. She believes that humans have an ontology, a deep reality that deserves awe. Beauty is a conversation between people and reality, and we must look for human dignity in the individual person (Robinson et al. 2023).

Soulfulness:
Soulfulness is about listening to the whispers of the soul. It is to wake up, be present, be awake and remember you are here just now. It is about stopping and being present in what is happening right now. It is about connection, a deeper contact with life, with other people and with God or a higher being. Draper says that when we look at someone in love we become part of a deeper consciousness, a divine shared consciousness. We reach out through the soul. It is a reminder that we belong to everything. Soulfulness is not floating on "a pink cloud". It is a down-to-earth, bodily way of embracing and transforming the world.

- What do you love doing?
- When do you feel most alive?
- What do you feel grateful for?
- What happens when you look at the world with love and compassion?

(From Brian Draper and Green (2020), a spiritual thinker from the UK)

The Soul and Nature

The Franciscan priest Richard Rohr (2013) believes that being in contact with nature is the best way to reconnect with the soul. It could be gardening, looking after animals, walks in woods and fields or many other things. It requires listening. Let "Sister Moon" and "Brother Dog" talk to you. We belong to this world and each other. The natural world is sacred. If we belong to something, we will respect, protect and love it.

Contact with nature can also help us cope with the often difficult work of a therapist. To enable us to listen and give, day after day, we need nourishment for our own souls. The ecological theologian Thomas Berry (2009) encourages us to stop, look and just listen:

> *What do you see? What do you see when you look up at the sky at night at the blazing stars against the midnight heavens? What do you see when the dawn breaks over the eastern horizon? What are your thoughts in the fading days of summer as the birds depart on their southward journey, or in autumn when the leaves turn brown and are blown away? What are your thoughts when you look out over the ocean in the evening? What do you see?*

Berry thinks we have lost our connection to the deeper reality of things. He says that reality often shows us that nothing is holy, nothing is sacred. Where is the wonder, the untouched, unspoiled and unused words? We consume the world and do not understand what this does to us. There is a need for a deep awareness of the sacred presence of the universe, a spirituality concerned with justice for humans and the larger community of the Earth.

LOVE

When was the last time you told someone you loved them? We are not thinking about partners or children, but everyone else you hang out with, friends, relatives or maybe clients. In our part of the world, language can be experienced as poor, correct and somewhat distant. There seem to be few people we let deeply into our hearts. At least this is rarely expressed in words.

We all need love. Love is essential for a good life. Love is a universal language and energy that goes beyond different religions or life ideologies. It is so simple that it is hard to say in words, but we all know it when we see it, and especially, feel it. Hopefully, love is home. Rohr (2018) says that love is a flow of energy willingly allowed and exchanged, without requiring payment in return. He finds that love allows and accommodates everything in human experience, both the good and the bad, and nothing else can really do this. Love flows unstoppably downward, around every obstacle—like water. Love is the energy that sustains the universe.

Axel Honneth (1995), well-known for his theory of recognition, says that love is fundamental for all people. If we do not receive care and love as children, we will struggle to develop emotional self-confidence. The

Bible verse "love your neighbour as yourself" implies respect for one's own integrity and an understanding that people need to be treated with respect, love and understanding. Loving someone means realizing your ability to love. The psychologist Erich Fromm (2006) has similar reflections and says that love of one person means at the same time love of people as a whole. He argues that the guarantee for one's own life, happiness and success is based on one's ability to love, i.e. to show care, respect, responsibility and insight. If we can only love others but not ourselves, we cannot love.

Sacred texts often refer to love; it is the cornerstone of many religions. The Bible tells us: *Keep thy heart with all diligence; for out of it are the issues of life* (Proverbs 4:23). The heart in this case is associated with courage, devotion, love and wisdom. A heart is more than a bodily organ that keeps a person alive. It pumps regularly and regulates our physical, psychological and spiritual well-being. In our western world, we focus strongly on the heart as the centre of everything, but the wisdom of traditions tells us that the heart has its own "brain" and is part of a larger whole. The heart has a greater perspective, and can see further, than the mind. We can call the heart our spiritual centre, as it is the core of imagination and intuition. In our heart we find our deepest desires and dreams. Trusting our heart is more than trusting our emotions. In our heart we find an invitation to let go or let be (Benner 2016).

Being able to show love is not a technique, something we "switch on" for therapy sessions. It is an attitude, a way of being, something to reach for in life.

Love is an important premise for the therapeutic dialogue. The Brazilian educator Paulo Freire (1979) believed that love was a source of power in relationships. This can give us an honest, liberating dialogue with a focus on what matters.

Suffering and Death

Life can be a tough journey at times, and we have probably all felt sad about something or someone we have lost or because life did not turn out as we had hoped. We all experience suffering. It is said that grief is the price of love, and our experiences can feel meaningless, like an infinite burden. However, suffering is part of life, also for clients. Our suffering will often affect our religious beliefs or spiritual life. Some turn their backs on God, others cling to God as a lifeline or a compass.

When we face death with our loved ones, it does something to us. We will not be the same as before. As we get older, we realize that we will not be young again. We know we are all mortal. Perhaps it will then be even more important to listen for what gives us meaning, hope, faith and good connections.

However, in a crisis, new dimensions in life often become more important. From experience, we know that many then become concerned with existential, spiritual or religious perspectives. Suffering seems to invite and lead us into the spiritual domain (Walsh 2009). In this way, whatever a person's belief or life philosophy, we can explore what the spiritual perspective means in suffering.

Spirituality and Suffering

Our experience is that it can be difficult to ask for spiritual perspectives, even in the midst of crisis and suffering. But the more we practice it, the more natural it becomes to us.

A woman who had lost several family members said that a text from the Book of Psalms became important to her:

Even though I walk through the valley of the shadow of death,
I will fear no evil,
for you are with me;
your rod and your staff,
they comfort me.
(Psalm 23, 4)

She reflected on the words rod and staff. What was the difference? She concluded that a rod was used to remove difficult feelings, while the staff was something to hold on to when the ground rocked beneath her.

Contemplation

As we have written, spirituality comes from the word spirit, which means breath. Breathing is something we do all the time without thinking about it. Yet we know that if our breathing stops, it is all over. In the same way that our body needs air, we believe our body needs a spiritual life force, which helps us find meaning and direction, and which can fill us with love.

Life is often busy, and so there is a need to stop sometimes to see the beauty and protect the goodness. We are part of the rhythm of life and ecosystem. A daily choice focusing on the good, the true and the beautiful is what we can call contemplation.

People do this in different ways. Some set aside time daily to just be quiet and breathe, some pray, others reflect on what creates gratitude, what makes life good. Some go for a walk in the woods, listen to the bird-song and discover the changes in nature. Others look out over the sea, looking for shells and listening to the roar of the waves. Such moments have no conclusion, but the point is to be quiet, nourish the soul and get in touch with one's inner life.

Deep Listening

If we are used to listening deeply, having contact with our inner life, it can help us in our work as a therapist. Systemic therapy focuses on language. Therapists and clients meet in dialogue. The heart of dialogue is a pro-found capacity to listen and be present.

Deep listening is not something we just switch on to, something instru-mental, a method that we use. Deep listening is, as we see it, a practice of being fully present—in heart, mind and body. It deepens our awareness and opens our hearts to love. It rewires us to meet and respond to reality as it is, without judgement or comparison (cac.org).

Sikh activist Valarie Kaur (2020) says:

Deep listening is an act of surrender. We risk being changed by what we hear. When I really want to hear another person's story, I try to leave my preconcep-tions at the door and draw close to their telling. I am always partially listening to my thoughts when others are speaking, so I consciously quiet my thoughts and begin to listen with my senses. … I try to understand what matters to them, not what I think matters. (pp. 143–144)

Kaur says that when the story is over, we have to return to "our skin", our worldview and notice how we have been changed by our visit. This can be very difficult, especially when people are very different from us. Can we try to understand without agreement?

Listening requires that we not only hear the words, but also embrace and accept, and gradually let go of our own inner clamouring. Listening is an expansive activity. It gives us a way to perceive more directly the ways we participate in the world around us. This means listening not only to others but also to ourselves and our reactions.

To listen deeply can be a difficult exercise. To listen is to develop an inner silence. This is not a familiar habit for most of us. We are talking about deep listening, on a digital and on an analogue level. It is about keeping all our senses open, while also keeping an eye on our own processes. Therefore, to listen requires receptivity, a willingness to be moved by the client. We are listening to the client and ourselves at the same time. How does the client's spiritual life affect me? Can I tolerate it, even if the client's spirituality is quite different from mine? I must be able to capture the feeling behind the client's words. If I can create an openness to the client's inner and outer spaces, I can be a co-creator of new growth and development.

The existential therapist Emmy Van Deurzen (2013) says that a phenomenological attitude can be of help in therapeutic settings. Here, we encourage a focus on people's lived experiences, what they see, hear, imagine, want, feel and do. This requires a stance of curiosity, openness and a wondering attitude, where we try to set aside our own biases or assumptions and look for the meaning from the client's perspective. Of course, we cannot put ourselves completely aside, with our values and assumptions about life, but we can be aware of this, which can help us become a better listener. A phenomenological perspective focuses on descriptions, explorations and meaning, and we must allow ourselves to stop, and not move forward too quickly. If the partners in the dialogue manage to listen to each other's perspectives, it can be of great help. New perspectives about each other that were completely unknown can emerge, and new meanings can arise. Acceptance and tolerance imply a non-judgemental attitude. We must try to accept and tolerate others' feelings and experiences. When clients receive such warmth and love, they can begin to see themselves through the therapist's eyes. The therapist does not evaluate the client's experience. The client is free to change or to let go.

An Example from Practice:
Peter asked for a therapy session because of his difficult marriage. His marriage had been difficult for decades. He very soon started talking about his childhood. He had grown up with a father who was a priest and a manic depressive, and a mother who had enough of herself. He said he had low self-esteem, calling it "my ugly back". Everything about faith became difficult for him as he grew up. The teaching did not match the life lived. As a teenager, he took a job in the church as a church warden. Then he could get paid, since he was forced to participate. He had recently managed to tell his mother that he was not a Christian, whereupon she burst into tears. This meant he was going to hell. We reflected on these perspectives, and he told how a humanistic view of people made sense to him. We talked about how the "ugly back" could get less space, and whether he could look for exceptions where his self-esteem was better than he assumed. When he returned, a month later, I met a different man. He seemed much happier and relieved, and he had discovered that his self-esteem was much better than he thought. He had contacted his siblings and an old friend, and even though his marriage might not survive, he knew he would do well anyway.

For this man, it was crucial to be able to talk about his childhood experiences of religion, which had influenced his adult life in various ways. He realized that religion did not have as much power over him as he thought. He felt free and could look for what gave him strength to take a new path.

Silence: A Good Teacher?

If we want to get in touch with our spirit, our inner life, our experience is that we need silence. However, silence can be experienced in at least two ways. We may experience turmoil and despair, but behind this, also peace. Silence may feel boring, and it is easy to want to do something else. Yet many people have found that if you have been restless, you encounter a light, a calm, a rest (Wickström 2007). In silence, we can listen and find out what gives us vitality, what makes life meaningful. Many people live stressful lives; we need a balance between rest, silence and activity.

However, our inner life can be nourished in various other ways. It could mean going for a walk in the woods, listening to music, going to an art exhibition, reading poetry, watching a film or writing, to name just a few possibilities. Where do I get new energy? What makes life meaningful? What is living? Where do I find what is good? We think we all need to ask ourselves such questions. How can we find boundaries and frameworks? How can we find light?

Contact with Our Body

As humans, we are also bodies. We experience the world through the body. All our experiences are stored in our body. Through our body we feel, act and reflect. The expression "the body remembers" is well-known, and when our body reacts, we can ask it what it is saying. As human beings, we are historically and culturally situated, and we communicate with our lifeworld. We try to create meaning, which is also a bodily process. By listening to our body, we get to know ourselves better. It is also necessary to help us face clients' various challenges, year after year. It will help us to be as open as possible to different topics, including spiritual and existential perspectives.

According to the phenomenologist of the body Merleau-Ponty (1962), our body longs for harmony, understanding and balance, and it tries to make contact with the world in various ways. We have some patterns that make us feel in harmony with the world. When these structures are challenged, we will not experience a dialogue with thoughts, words and feelings, and the body will then try to create meaning. The body will "say something".

Love Your Body!
If we want to listen to our body, we should also take care of it. In a time like ours, it is very easy to be critical of our body. But how can we be happy in our own body? When we meet our clients, we are also bodies. A negative body image will be noticeable. How can we be grateful for our body—and relate to it with joy? We know the body needs healthy food, movement, touch and rest. We need contact with our body, and to get to know it. We need to be in tune with ourselves and our body's needs. Then our body will take us out into the world with renewed energy.
(Øiestad 2009)

Reflections

---

1. What is your first memory of a spiritual or religious encounter?
   - What kind of feelings does it arouse in you?
   - What does this experience mean to you now?
2. What does it mean to you to live a spiritual life?
3. How can the soul get small spaces in everyday life?
4. Apart from your closest relationships, when was the last time you said you loved someone?
5. Take a break, and give thanks to your body. Close your eyes, and feel the breath and vibration that go through your body. Put your hands on your stomach, take a deep breath of life energy and let it spread throughout your body, from your head to your toes, and especially where it is most needed.
6. - Think of the word spirituality and write everything you feel.
   - Choose two words from what you have written and write more about these two words.
   - Finally, reflect on what this might mean for you.
7. Take a moment to think about your life and your death. What meaning has your life held? What has been important to you during your journey? What do you want people to remember about you? What are the footprints you leave behind in this world?

REFERENCES

Benner, D. G. (2016). *Human being and becoming: living the adventure of life and love*. Brazos Press, a division of Baker Publishing Group.

Berry, T. (2009). *The sacred universe: earth, spirituality, and religion in the twenty-first century*. Columbia University Press.

Corbett, L. (2011). *The Sacred Cauldron: psychotherapy as a spiritual practice*. Chiron.

Draper, B., & Green, H. (2020). *Soulful nature: a spiritual field guide*. Canterbury Press.

Freire, P. (1979). *Pedagogy of the oppressed*. Sheed and Ward.

Fromm, E. (2006). *The art of loving* (Fiftieth anniversary ed.). Harper Perennial.

Honneth, A. (1995). *The struggle for recognition: the moral grammar of social conflicts*. Polity Press.

Kaur, V. (2020). *See no stranger: a memoir and manifesto of revolutionary love* (First edition.). One World.

McLaren, B. D. (2016). *The Great Spiritual Migration: How the World's Largest Religion Is Seeking a Better Way to Be Christian*. The Crown Publishing Group.

Merleau-Ponty, M. (1962). *Phenomenology of perception*. Routledge.

Plotkin, B. (2003). *Soulcraft: Crossing into the Mysteries of Nature and Psyche*. New World Library.

Roach, M. (2003). *Stiff: the curious lives of human cadavers* (Large print ed.). Thorndike Press.

Robinson, M., Robinson, M., & Jordal, P. (2023). *Hva gjør vi her?: en essaysamling om litteratur, språk og teologi*. Verbum.

Rohr, R. (2011). *Falling upward: a spirituality for the two halves of life*. Jossey-Bass.

Rohr, R. (2013). *Immortal diamond: the search for our true self*. SPCK.

Rohr, R. (2018). *Richard Rohr: essential teachings on love*. ORBIS books.

Rohr, R. (2019). *The universal Christ: how a forgotten reality can change everything we see, hope for and believe*. SPCK, Society for Promoting Christian Knowledge; Convergent Books.

Van Deurzen, E. (2013). *Existential Perspectives on Relationship Therapy*. Palgrave Macmillan. http://public.eblib.com/choice/publicfullrecord.aspx?p=4008556

Walsh, F. (2009). *Spiritual resources in family therapy*. Guilford Press.

Wickström, O. (2007). *Det bländande mörkret. Att upptäcka den stora glädjen*. Libris.

Øiestad, G. (2009). *Selvfølelsen*. Gyldendal.

CHAPTER 7

Existential Psychotherapy and Existential Health

The seven wonders of the world:
To see, to hear, to touch, to taste,
To feel, to laugh—and to love

What can we learn from other traditions? Let us take a closer look at what is called "Existential psychotherapy", a tradition that is concerned with existential and spiritual perspectives, and sees these as the core of therapeutic work. Virginia Satir, one of the mothers of family therapist, wanted to link existential perspectives with systemic practice. We will also take a closer look at the term "existential health", which has been developed in the wake of existential therapy. There seems to be a need for a concept broader and deeper than "mental health", a term that can better capture people's existential lives.

EXISTENTIAL PSYCHOTHERAPY

Originally the term "psychology" comes from *psyche*, which means "soul", and *logos*, which means "teaching", i.e. "the study of the soul" (Reed 1998).

A psychotherapeutic approach that seems to take the soul seriously is existential psychotherapy. The Norwegian psychologist and professor of psychology Per Einar Binder (2023) says:

© The Author(s), under exclusive license to Springer Nature
Switzerland AG 2024
Å. Holmberg, P. Jensen, *Working with Spirituality in Family
Systemic Practice*, Palgrave Texts in Counselling and Psychotherapy,
https://doi.org/10.1007/978-3-031-77310-5_7

Existential psychotherapy is a pluralistic tradition with a background in existential philosophy and humanistic, experiential and psychodynamic therapy traditions. A basic premise is that psychological difficulties arise when we encounter difficulties in dealing with emotional pain that is at once specific to our own individual lives, and at the same time related to common human concerns.

Existential psychotherapy has the unique human lifeworld as its starting point. This approach is dialogical and tries to understand people's conflicts and challenges in their everyday existence. Van Deurzen and Iacovou (2013) argues that existential psychotherapy is the only established form of psychotherapy that is directly based on philosophy. The therapy is based on the client's ontological descriptions of life and links them to reflection on the meaning of life. The aim is a dialogical conversation with the tensions in the clients' lives, to acknowledge the paradoxes and find a new direction. Here clients' meaning-making, values and beliefs are included. Doubt and wonder can both help to strengthen people's self-reflection and enable them to move forward on their life path. Von Deurzen says that people in postmodern society struggle with meaninglessness, which can manifest itself in a multitude of problems.

Human beings seem to easily lose their sense of direction. Von Deurzen believes that the psychotherapy tradition in general found it difficult to accept philosophical questions and see the importance for clients to dwell on them. In order to do this, she says that therapists must ask themselves such questions and be able to face their anxiety and meaninglessness.

In this tradition, people are seen as co-owners of their personality and have the ability to choose, prioritize and also opt out. How we act defines us as people. We also have to accept the consequences of our actions. The focus in existential therapy is on exploration, recognition and dialogue. The aim is to create greater insight into one's reflections and life situations. The Norwegian doctor Anders Malkomsen (Malkomsen and Malkomsen 2023) says that existential therapy is based on the idea that all people have the psychological freedom to choose who they want to be and that we therefore have a responsibility for who we are and what we do with our lives. This includes a recognition that we are all mortal, and that is why the choices we make are so important—while we are still alive.

As humans, we also have to deal with bodily limitations. The body can give us many pleasures, joys and opportunities, but at the same time, it also limits freedom. Despite our relationships, in this tradition, there is an acknowledgement that no one will ever fully understand us. We live our innermost lives alone—and we die alone. As for the question of meaning, it is pointed out that nothing matters if it does not make sense to us.

Existential psychotherapy claims to have a holistic approach, with the human being intertwined with the world in their relationships (van Deurzen and Iacovou 2013). Crises and suffering are part of life, and both anxiety and the feeling of discomfort can lead us towards necessary change. The good life does not come by itself. Each person is unique and valuable and has the capacity and opportunity to work on their situation and find new directions in life.

In existential psychotherapy, difficulties in life are not seen as an illness. Diagnoses are rejected as tools for understanding mental disorders. Here, the focus is on self-knowledge, insight and acquired wisdom. Aristotle's concept of *phronesis*, which means practical wisdom and knowledge from lived life, is encouraged. Everyone should find their own way of living, their truth. This fits well with a social constructionist way of thinking. The Swedish existential therapist Elisabeth Serrander (2018) argues that that we are born into a situation that we have not chosen, a world, a body, family, culture and context, and this will mark us during our life's journey. At the same time, we have the freedom to transcend our reality, the ability to change, the capacity to repair and act differently, freedom to choose. Existential psychotherapy asserts that life is an uncertain project. We are all going to die and we are constantly changing, both to ourselves, others and the world at large. But we all have a certain freedom. The meaning of life is to exist and to constantly innovate through our choices, our will and our power to act (Serrander 2018).

Existential therapy is inspired by phenomenology, through reaching into the "things" in themselves—without interpreting or explaining. This can create awareness in the client. The client's life world is explored, including the physical, personal, social and spiritual aspects (van Deurzen and Iacovou 2013). The goal is for clients to be actors in the life that is their own, and to live as authentically and meaningfully as possible. The physical perspective is about our relationship to the body, to nature, to time and space and to the material. The personal perspective is about our relationship with ourselves, our identity and life history, our feelings and judgements. The social is about our relationships to culture, to society and its norms, to people and animals. The spiritual, in this context, is about our faith, religion, philosophy of life, values and opinions and is considered decisive for how the other perspectives are lived (van Deurzen and Iacovou 2013).

Reflections about Practice
As we see it, one of the big differences between systemic therapy and existential therapy is that in the latter one has a clear idea of what the focus should be in therapy. In systemic therapy, we are more open to what clients bring to the session, but we still believe there can be perspectives to learn from existential psychotherapy. The most important thing is the natural involvement of existential perspectives and to see this dimension as crucial to living a meaningful life.

We can also ask ourselves whether it would have been wise to have a clearer agenda. Narrative therapy has a clear recipe, and integrative therapy is also concerned with this. Had the spiritual dimension come in more naturally, if problems were to be explored in a physical, psychological, social and spiritual perspective?

EXISTENTIAL HEALTH

Let us move on to a term that has emerged in the West in recent times, namely existential health (DeMarinis 2008). The word spiritual health does not seem to be used so much, although we interpret the terms as two of a kind.

Existential health may be defined as follows:

Existential health is having a basic sense of security and belonging in the world, that enables people to create, in everyday living, a sense of meaning of and for themselves and of life, and contributes to the ability to deal with crises and ultimate questions of life. (DeMarinis 2008; Lloyd 2018)

The World Health Organization describes health as a state of complete physical, mental and social well-being, not merely the absence of disease or infirmity (https://www.who.int/about/governance/constitution). Several people have advocated that this concept of health should be expanded with a spiritual/existential dimension.

A group within the WHO has conducted a pilot study in 18 countries on how spiritual, religious and personal beliefs relate to health-related quality of life (Group 2006). This resulted in eight perspectives which they believe are important for people's existential health:

1. Harmony and inner peace
2. Experience of context
3. Existential strength and power
4. Trust as life force
5   Meaning of life
6   Experience of wholeness
7   Experience of wonder
8. Hope

The absence of life pain is an ideal state that is impossible to achieve. To live is a result of our confrontation with the basic conditions of life such as the human relationship to meaning, vulnerability, loneliness, death, freedom, responsibility, guilt and belonging. This is not necessarily pathological. There is a danger of pathologizing this existential and constructive experience of pain in a culture where discomfort is easily defined as illness.

The term "existential health" can be fruitful because it incorporates aspects such as faith, a sense of dignity, hope, meaning, connection, spirituality and the ability to handle crises. The term provides a pluralistic experience of what good health is and increases our ability to reflect on and take a stand for our values.

Existential health means embracing life in all its complexity. It involves finding meaning and hope, taking an active and responsible attitude towards life with the opportunities and limitations that make up our human existence. Binder argues that we might become healthier through our existential struggles because meaning is essential for a healthy life (Binder 2022). But at the deepest level, we do not face our existential challenges to become healthy. Binder says we struggle because meaning and existential concerns are of the highest value to our lives.

People's existential health affects physical, mental and social health. Everything is connected. In a systemic perspective, it may be important to explore how these perspectives are connected and influence each other. Family members can also experience this differently, which can be important to clarify.

Nevertheless, linking existential perspectives to the concept of health has also been criticized. There seems to be little research related to the term from clinical practice, and this promotes only positive aspects and thus becomes too narrow for people's lives in general. Doubt, restlessness, hopelessness, weakness and loneliness can also be part of life, and one cannot promise that these will be "solved" by therapy (Stiwne 2018). People's life problems are also linked to the society we are part of, and what kind of help public health care offers.

Mental health care is now under great pressure, as package procedures, pills and diagnoses are often not the best help for this type of person. People are also co-creators of their own problems, and from an existential point of view, actively participate in helping to change their own situation. Stiwne believes that existential life problems and dilemmas should not be defined within the framework of health care and health services. By turning existential health into an additional health concept, one risks blurring the lines between life problems and what is today called mental illness. Different ways of living do not need to be pathologized and legitimized in a medical, diagnostic perspective. Stiwne therefore suggests dividing the term and talking about existence AND health. However, from our point of view, we feel that it is inappropriate for the medical model to have a monopoly on the concept of health. We prefer a holistic concept of health, which includes various parts of a relational human life.

Reflections on Existential Philosophical Perspectives

What can we learn from the philosophy of existentialism? The Norwegian psychologist Schibbye (2006) describes it as exploring our awareness of life. She says that increasing our life awareness is about being open to our inner life, and living close to emotions such as vitality, passion, calm and joy. The goal is to be touched by the experience of living right now and to be more present in our own lives.

We only live once. At least here on earth. Lives are filled with joy and sorrow, longing and pain. Existential philosophy teaches us to process these experiences, not run away.

What is the meaning of life? Why am I here? What happens when I die? These are questions existential philosophers want us to ponder—and find answers to.

We know we exist. Life can be wonderful. But we also know that life is vulnerable. We could be dead tomorrow. Life is about experiences, sometimes difficult to put into words. We are part of something bigger and no one really knows what it is. We can just believe in something and open ourselves to the inner voices so we can live as authentically as possible.

Listening to the inner voices can make us restless. Therefore, many people fill their lives with noise and various activities. We can escape from the existential part of life. Our identity can be based on external roles and characteristics. Then we can lose ourselves on the way. Moods and feelings can arise in us. Then we are close to what Heidegger (1982) calls our being. As human beings, we are irreplaceable. No one is quite like you or me. Human beings exist before they are given substance. We are in constant motion, and we become. This acknowledgement is necessary for self-reflection, according to Schibbye. The philosophy of existence can inspire us to discover new sides of ourselves. It makes us ask questions about the meaning of life and whether we are taking care of the only life we were given here on earth. It calls on us to search inward, into the atmosphere that fills us—and to follow it.

We may all have been in situations we can call soulless. Superficial meetings, a feeling of emptiness. Words have lost passion and power; we are pawns in a context that we perceive as meaningless. Yet we are encouraged to set boundaries and take responsibility for our own life, live a conscious life. This is freedom in the existential sense. We have the opportunity to choose.

In existential philosophy, anxiety is described as human, an unpleasant feeling that can seem paralysing. Yet anxiety is also an opportunity to get closer to ourselves and our spiritual life. In anxiety we approach our existence. Anxiety tells us that there is something we are repressing, something unseen that is fading away in me.

Anxiety is linked to death. We are not immortal, and we are moving ever closer to our own death. People can rush around, trying to forget their own mortality. The existentialists want us to stop and listen to the experiences that come to us. They encourage us to wonder, to play and to be creative. It is in experiences that we change. We cannot rationalize away our anxiety. If we achieve a conscious relationship with our anxiety, we think we can become less vulnerable, freer and more responsible in our choices. If we are in anxiety, we can try to access some answers from our inner self. Death goes hand in hand with life. Awareness of death protects us from wrong priorities and goals that lead in the wrong direction. It is important to live before death occurs.

By seeing ourselves, we can also see others. This is connected to our capacity for love. Love is a feeling, a force, an experience, something mysterious. Love is between us and others. Charity is existential, the deepest ground of spiritual life. In love we live and breathe. The source of love lies in the depths. Existential love is not selfish, but quietly waits for me to open up. It manifests itself in loving actions. We come into being in the resonance of the other's love. Love gives others the right to themselves, their experiences, feelings, thoughts and opinions. It is about recognition of the other. It is expressed in our language and in our actions. Being understood builds love. We believe we must open ourselves to love—and let it take its place. In the presence of existence I see more clearly, and I find home (Schibbye 2006).

An existential perspective means that we are always in relationships, and we are all shaped by the relations we are part of. We are always in a context, always connected to what is around us. Our relationships are crucial and inspire everything we do (van Deurzen and Iacovou 2013).

VIRGINIA SATIR: COMBINING SYSTEMIC THINKING AND EXISTENTIALISM

One of the pioneers in the systemic family therapy field, Virginia Satir, wanted to include existentialism in her systemic work (Satir 1991). She was inspired by philosophers such as Sören Kierkegaard, Martin Buber and Johann Heidegger. She believed that human beings were bearers of positive life energy, which could be transformed into a high level of self-care in the context of high self-esteem. Love was important to her, and she said that people need something that validates the self. She helped people to find what she called their "wisdom book", a sense of worth, acceptance of self, hope, empowerment and an ability to be responsible for their own lives and make choices. She wanted clients to focus on their uniqueness and encouraged them to look appreciatively at all parts of themselves, using them to grow and to become more fully human (p. 4).

Satir's theoretical framework states that all humans are equal, and the biggest obstacle to peace between humans is that people do not know how to perceive their equality of value. She believed that every human has an inborn spiritual base and sacredness, and displays a universal life force.

Satire argues that all humans have an "essence", which includes values, beliefs and assumptions, and which appears in feelings, perceptions, expectations and yearning. Satir believed that people, like icebergs, only show part of themselves, and that most experiences lie beneath the surface. To know one's true self, one must enter the subconscious and pass through many hidden parts (Koca 2017). Satir says we are connected to our universal essence, and we have the ability to achieve a new universal consciousness and peace, despite many previous difficult experiences in life.

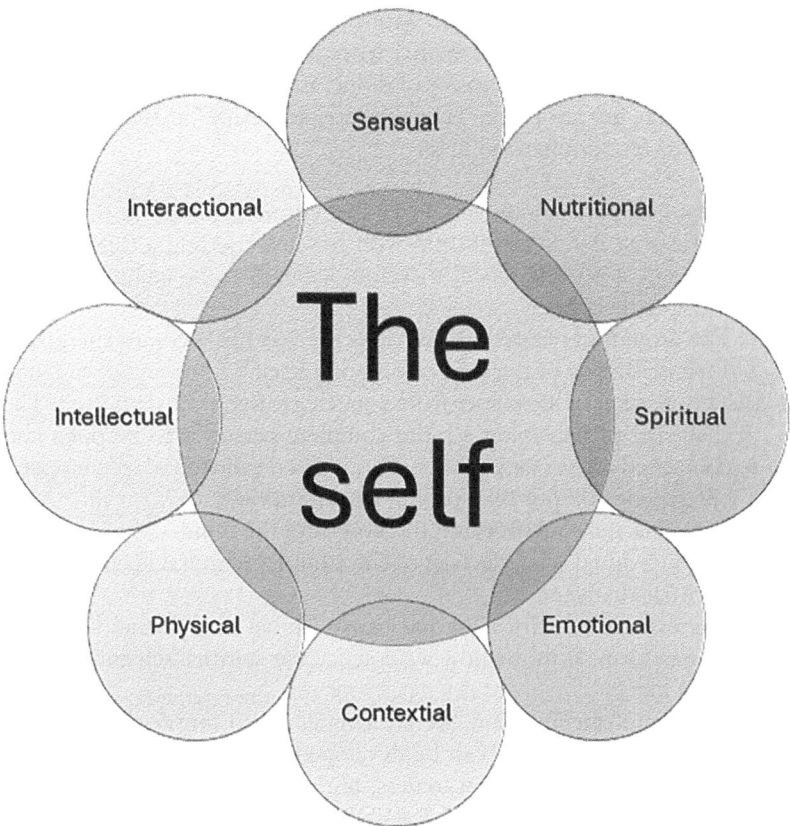

Fig. 7.1 Satir's model: "The self mandala"

Humans also have longings. Satir says that each person is longing to be loved, accepted, validated and appreciated. She developed a holistic concept called the "self mandala" (see Fig. 7.1). It is a picture of every human being, a sacred person with a holy self. Satir says that every human is housed in a temple, i.e. their body, which needs nourishment. We have an intellectual part, and we have feelings, emotions and senses. As human beings we are always connected, we are part of a context which always has time, movement, colour, temperature and air of some sort. Finally, the life source of human spirituality is a universal energy which connects us with each other and with the energy of the universe.

All parts of us affect each other. Satir developed and deepened a way of seeing people with a great potential to maximize their inner resources, their self-esteem and their choices of doing and being. Shortly before she died, she wrote her last book, "The new peoplemaking" (Satir 1988), and her thoughts are summarized here:

1. We are all part of a universal tree that connects people at the roots.
2. Spirituality is our connection with the universe and a fundamental element of our existence; therefore it needs to be included in this therapeutic context.
3. The growth of plants and animals is the way life becomes energized, a manifestation of the soul manifesting itself.
4. The creation of life comes from a much greater force than itself. The challenge of becoming a more complete person is to be open and connected to its many names. This is often called God. A successful life depends on our relationship with this power.
5. Crushing the soul, freezing the body and the mind.
6. The individual is a reflection of the ethical and moral ideals of one's spiritual character.
7. The essence of spirituality has us realize we are spiritual beings in human form. It shows how we practice our spiritual self and how we value life.
8. Thanks to our intuition, we are connected to universal consciousness. These intuitions can be developed with meditation, worship, relaxation techniques, awareness, high self-esteem, and respect for life. This is a spiritual approach. (Satir 1988)

What we can learn from Virginia Satir is, how we see it, that when someone enters our therapy room, each person is special, a gift, with their uniqueness. We are part of something greater that we cannot see. There can be healing powers beyond what we can see, which can enhance the healing process.

The word heal is not the same as cure. To cure is to remove an affliction or a disease. We think healing has to do with the wholeness of people. To heal is to feel whole, be allowed to be who I am, be able to use one's resources and feel meaning (Myskja 2015).

Reflections

1. What do you think we can learn from existential psychotherapy?
2. Do you have other sources that inspire you to include spirituality in your work?
3. In what way can the concept of existential health be of help in psychotherapeutic work?

REFERENCES

Binder, P.-E. (2022). Suffering a Healthy Life-On the Existential Dimension of Health. *Frontiers in psychology, 13,* 803792–803792.

Binder, P.-E. (2023). Eksistensiell psykoterapi. *Tidsskrift for Norsk psykologforening, 60*(12), 831–840. https://doi.org/10.52734/VFBM1057

DeMarinis, V. (2008). The impact of postmodernization on existential health in Sweden: Psychology of religion's function in existential public health analysis. *Archive for the Psychology of Religion, 30*(1), 57–74.

Deurzen, E. van. & Iacovou, S. (2013). *Existential perspectives on relationship therapy.* Palgrave Macmillan. http://public.eblib.com/choice/publicfullrecord. aspx?p=4008556

Group, W. S. (2006). A cross-cultural study of spirituality, religion, and personal beliefs as components of quality of life. *Social science & medicine (1982), 62*(6), 1486–1497. https://doi.org/10.1016/j.socscimed.2005.08.001

Heidegger, M. (1982). *On the way to language.* HarperOne.

Koca, D. A. (2017). Spirituality-based analysis of Satir family therapy. *Spiritual Psychology and Counseling, 2*(2), 121–142.

Lloyd, C. (2018). *Moments of meaning–Towards an assessment of protective and risk factors for existential vulnerability among young women with mental ill-health concerns: A mixed methods project in clinical psychology of religion and existential health* Acta Universitatis Upsaliensis].

Malkomsen, A., & Malkomsen, A. (2023). *Hva er poenget?: om meningsløshetens psykologi og eksistensielle samtaler* (1. utgave. ed.). Fagbokforlaget.

Myskja, A. (2015). *Helbred deg selv: styrk din egen motstandskraft.* Stenersen.

Reed, E. S. (1998). *From soul to mind: The emergence of psychology from Erasmus Darwin to William James.* Yale University Press.

Satir, V. (1988). *The new peoplemaking.* Science and Behavior Books.

Satir, V. (1991). *The Satir model: family therapy and beyond.* Science and Behavior Books.

Schibbye, A.-L. L. (2006). *Livsbevissthet: om å være til stede i eget liv.* Universitetsforl.

Serrander, E. (2018). När kroppen visar vägen. In D. Stiwne (Ed.), *Existens och psykisk hälsa* (pp. 65–87). Studentlitteratur.

Stiwne, D. (2018). *Existens och psykisk hälsa: om hur liv och levnad förhåller sig till hälsa och ohälsa.* Studentlitteratur.

CHAPTER 8

Developing Spiritual Literacy in Dialogical Practice

Stepping into the presence of a soulful person is like entering a
beautiful café, an art gallery or a shrine.
—*Brian Draper*

In the previous chapter, we went into more detail about how we can develop our own spiritual journey and become better at listening to clients' spiritual perspectives. We have also looked more closely at existentialism and seen how existential philosophical approaches can add valuable perspectives to the systemic field.

We will now move towards a theory, developed through a PhD study (Holmberg 2018), which was called "A map of spiritual and existential literacy in systemic practice". The theory helps systemic practitioners to develop spiritual and existential literacy in systemic therapy. But first, we will dwell on the term literacy, a term little used in systemic practice. We will also delve into the concept of resonance, which we see as a prerequisite for spiritual and existential literacy.

Å. Holmberg, P. Jensen, *Working with Spirituality in Family
Systemic Practice*, Palgrave Texts in Counselling and Psychotherapy,
https://doi.org/10.1007/978-3-031-77310-5_8

What Does the Concept of Literacy Mean?

A general definition of literacy is the ability to read and write. It is to be literate, which also means having knowledge or skill in a specified field (https://en.oxforddictionaries.com/definition/literacy). The everyday meaning is strictly verbal, cognitive or mental; we may think it has to do with words and the verbal skills of reading and writing. In our case, we need to consider the deeper meaning of the concept. A more inclusive definition can be to recognize the meaning in certain shapes, signs and marks. It is the ability to pick up meaning and intention through tone of voice, facial expression and body language. It is the ability to "read" and sense in human relations, it is about being present and awake bodily, and about the ability to reach deep levels in the human mind (Dictionary.com).

In a systemic world, literacy is a relational concept because we define humans as relational and believe that learning occurs in a relationship with others. In addition, just as we need letters to learn to read and write, a person also needs some general knowledge to be a literate therapist. That does not mean that this general knowledge applies to everyone, but therapists may need knowledge of different dimensions of human life.

A human being, including the body, can be compared to a text, and this metaphor is used in different contexts. One example is from Andres Piltz (1991), who says that man is like a script, whose content is open only for humans with literacy. Pär Lagerkvist (1959), a Swedish author, compared the face of a human with a book:

> Wondering and searching, he entered into this dark, furrowed face, as he wanted to read this ancient book, which despite its clear signage was difficult to read. It looked like it was written in an old-fashioned language, which no one spoke anymore. (p. 10)

There are multiple varieties of humans as texts, varieties of styles and language. To read the human is about exploring its meaning and deeper motives. The text becomes a metaphor for a deeper context of meaning. Piltz (1991) says, "There is a tension between the author and the text; the letters can be killed by humans; the text may become a paling (fence) of letters that block communication" (p. 55). In each encounter, we must seek the unique, be awake and open to the individual client. There is a connection between the text, the story and the reader, and in the dialogue, the text can be framed and rewritten (Eriksson et al. 2003).

Words and language are fundamental to human beings; they are how we think and relate to others. Words, texts and language enable us to find a meaningful way in life. In the spoken word, humans turn to each other; in speech, words become alive (Eriksson et al. 2003).

The concept of literacy is used in different contexts. We can talk about democratic literacy, economic literacy, methodological literacy, religious literacy and spiritual literacy. The word literacy has not been used much in the family therapy field, but we find it relevant because of the great concern in the field with language and communication, collaborative practice, the concept of "not-knowing" and the focus on meeting clients with respect and acknowledgement. The clinical psychologist and family therapist Peter Rober (2005) is concerned with what he calls "the dialogical self" and says that we have to meet clients with both receptivity and reflection. As therapists, we have to be aware of our experiences and inner conversations to enable them to inform and enrich the therapeutic conversation.

ARE WE OPEN TO SPIRITUAL LITERACY?

After delving into the concept of literacy, it will be natural to go further and ask: How can we develop *spiritual literacy* in systemic practice?

If we are serious about wanting to be therapists who encourage dialogue and collaboration, there can be no closed topics. We have to show that we are open to clients' spiritual perspectives. The clients in our study said that they could easily sense whether therapists were open or not to their spiritual life. Here is one example from the client Julia:

Julia   *The therapist did not understand. He said, 'So what?', and for me, it was very strange. I felt that he couldn't understand my Christian background, that even such a cruel man is hard to leave, because it's wrong in a way ... And I felt it was something about our connection, because this 'room' is so big in my life, and with the therapist, I needed to close the door. I could talk about everything else, there were thousands of things, but I felt it wasn't fruitful to continue.*

Interviewer   *And this 'room' is, as you say, quite big?*

Julia   *For me, it's very big, yes, it infiltrates everything; it infiltrates who I am as a person, and ... I just felt that a door was closed, you know; he did not understand me at all. I felt I was a problem.*

The therapists also talked about situations where spirituality was "out of bounds" and was described as not fitting in with systemic therapy:

> *Normally, when we come up with such an interpretation, we are seen as a bit exotic, but sometimes also perhaps that we are not normal. Some people think this is just nonsense. And especially, many people think it is unprofessional. So in the same way as the clients ... when they enter the therapy room, they do not point out that this is a type of spiritual thinking. They test the therapist by coming up with keywords, and ... and if the therapist hangs on, they can continue. Of course, we do the same as (them) ... we quickly realize when ... professionals, therapists, either shake their heads or roll their eyes or somehow show that this is so uninteresting and unprofessional. "Let's get back to business!" Then we stop talking about it ... We react in the same way as the clients do.*

In these examples, we see that clients and therapists hold back when they feel the topic is not being acknowledged. They are holding back something that is vitally important in their lives.

Reflections about Practice
Holding back is perhaps something that we have all experienced from time to time. It can be about the therapy situation, among colleagues or in guidance. What is it that makes us hold back, even something that we feel is important? Is it fear? Are we afraid of not being taken seriously, that we will be attacked or have to defend ourselves?

Searching for the concept of "spiritual literacy", we found two contributions from the field of psychotherapy. The first is from Haug (1998a, 1998b), who argues that spiritual literacy is a non-judgemental and respectful attitude to clients' spiritual and religious issues, tuning in with the language of clients and working for change through the inclusion of clients' beliefs and values. She says that this depends on therapists' sensitivity, spiritual knowledge and self-awareness of the topic and their ability to cooperate with the clients and consider their right to self-determination. Haug's reflections fit well with the second theoretical contribution from psychotherapist Kenneth Pargament (2007), who states that spiritually integrated psychotherapy is grounded in spiritual literacy and competence on the part of the therapist, and it goes beyond personal spirituality to a well-integrated professional spiritual perspective. For Pargament, it includes spiritual knowledge, openness and tolerance, self-awareness and authenticity. The key is not only to have knowledge of spirituality but also to have the wisdom of how to introduce this knowledge into therapy in collaboration with clients.

RESONANCE

We will now go to the concept of resonance. Resonance is both a physical and a musical concept. Here we use the concept resonance as a metaphor. The sociologist Hartmut Rosa calls it the moment when the world sings. Resonance is produced only when the vibration of one body stimulates the other to produce its frequency (Rosa 2019). Therefore, resonance is a kind of relationship with the world, formed through emotions and interests. It is not an echo, but a responsive relationship, where both sides speak with their voice but are also open enough to be affected or reached by each other.

Rosa defines resonance as follows:

> The concept of resonance … is (1) metaphorically the basic affective state of a healthy person who is authentically in sync with him—or herself in as many aspects of his or her personality as possible and (2) descriptive of a phenomenon in which multiple people are in sync with each other, primarily nonverbally. (Rosa 2019, p. 167)

The concept of resonance has been developed to include parallel connections, which is what occurs when a client or a family communicates and presents narratives that remind the therapist of her or his own personal and private experiences. This awareness is not only intellectual and possibly outside conscious awareness, but also embodied and emotional. The resonance we are studying here involves two aspects: a family therapist's personal and private life and her or his professional life. The emphasis on resonance will be developed to include several related concepts that add new meaning to the findings from this research project (Jensen 2012).

How can we give resonance to a client's spiritual life? How can we explain resonance? When a client or a family meets a therapist, resonance takes place between the family or client and the therapist. The resonance may be emotional, cognitive or contextual, or indeed a mixture of all three. The resonance might be very strong and dominating or in a milder form at all levels. These processes will be part of how we might understand the therapy (Jensen 2008).

The Belgian family therapist Money Elkaïm (1941–2020) introduced the concept of resonance to help us understand the dynamics between how one part of life may influence another. He says: "Resonance occurs when the same rule or feeling appears to be present in different but related systems" (Elkaïm 1997, p. xxvii). What occurs then is a kind of symmetry that invites the person to relate in certain ways or in similar ways to what is taking place. Resonance is thus a concept for giving meaning to the circularity that occurs between the therapist's life and clients' narratives (Elkaïm 1997).

Martha Rogers broadens the understanding of resonance by presenting it in a relational perspective. She argues that resonance with the environment may sometimes be "harmonic, sometimes cacophonous, sometimes dissonant" (Rogers 1970, p. 219).

Relational resonance also includes personal resonance. This means that resonance not only takes place in the therapist's mind and emotions (personal resonance), and in the individual family members' minds, but also between the therapist and the family or client (Jensen 2012).

As humans, we are created for resonance. We need security, protection and care. That is what attachment theory has taught us. We know that our emotional and social development is affected by how we are met and received (Dallos and Vetere 2021). We mutually create each other. We think the ability for resonance is under pressure in our society. This pressure can lead to alienation and an exhaustion of the self, where relationships become instrumental. Seikkula (2008) notes that a surprising number of professionals find it difficult to be in dialogue with clients and colleagues.

Many professionals seem to be most concerned with being proficient in different methods and interventions, which can take the focus away from the basic idea of being present in the moment and letting all voices be heard. If resonance is part of the solution, we think it is initially about bringing oneself into play as an instrument in relational interactions (Tønder and Karlsson 2020).

As systemic therapists, we bring with us our own experience and history, and this will probably have a great influence on what we choose to emphasize in the dialogue (Jensen 2008). If spiritual perspectives are foreign to us, both personally and professionally, there is a high probability that we will not give resonance to these dimensions of the clients' lives. The therapist's values, interests and personal experiences will create a context for the therapeutic work. However, the ability to resonate and establish connections and responsive relationships can be trained and refined. As therapists, we believe we need to ask ourselves if we are a door-opener or a door-closer to the client's spiritual room. Knowing there is space can make a difference to the client (Holmberg et al. 2017).

Resonance might occur when people share narratives, and it might occur when they share feelings. Resonance is about both telling stories and showing emotions. Resonance is found both in interaction between people and between myself and my stories and emotions.

We have here presented and examined two central concepts for our understanding of spirituality in family therapy practice, namely literacy and resonance. To link these two concepts together, we believe therapists need to use their curiosity to gain a deeper understanding of the meaning of spirituality in a specific family. Family therapists might have more or less knowledge and practice from their own spiritual life. However, we think it is always necessary for the therapist to use curiosity to reach a deeper understanding of spirituality in a specific family or client.

Reflections

---

1. What are your experiences of spiritual literacy?
2. How do you listen to your heart's calling?
3. Think about your life: Can you remember a story when you experienced resonance with your spiritual life?

REFERENCES

Dallos, R., & Vetere, A. (2021). *Systemic therapy and attachment narratives: Applications in a range of clinical settings.* Routledge.

Elkaïm, M. (1997). *If you love me, don't love me: undoing reciprocal double binds and other methods of change in couple and family therapy.* J. Aronson.

Eriksson, K., Lindström, U. Å., & Åbo akademi Institutionen för, v. (2003). *Gryning: II: Klinisk vårdvetenskap* (Vol. II). Institutionen för vårdvetenskap, Åbo Akademi.

Haug, I. (1998a). Including a spiritual dimension in family therapy: Ethical considerations. *Contemporary family therapy, 20*(2), 181–194.

Haug, I. (1998b). Spirituality as a Dimension of Family Therapists' Clinical Training. *Contemporary family therapy, 20*(4), 471–483. https://doi.org/1 0.1023/A:1021628132514

Holmberg, Å. (2018). *Making room for spirituality?: family therapists' and clients' perceptions and experiences about spirituality in family therapy* VID Specialized University]. Oslo.

Holmberg, Å., Jensen, P., & Ulland, D. (2017). To Make Room or Not to Make Room: Clients' Narratives About Exclusion and Inclusion of Spirituality in Family Therapy Practice. *Australian and New Zealand Journal of Family Therapy, 38*(1), 15–26. https://doi.org/10.1002/anzf.1198

Jensen, P. (2008). *The Narratives which connect...: a qualitative research approach to the Narratives which connect therapists' personal and private lives to their family therapy practices.* University of East London]. London.

Jensen, P. (2012). Family Therapy, Personal Life and Therapeutic Practice. The Map of Relational Resonance as a Language for Analyzing Psychotherapeutic Processes. *Human Systems: The Journal of Therapy, Consultation & Training, 23*(1), 68–87.

Lagerkvist, P. (1959). *Sibyllan.* Bonnier.

Pargament, K. I. (2007). *Spiritually integrated psychotherapy: understanding and addressing the sacred.* Guilford Press.

Piltz, A. (1991). *Mellan ängel och best: människans värdighet och gåta i europeisk tradition.* Alfabeta.

Rober, P. (2005). The Therapist's Self in Dialogical Family Therapy: Some Ideas About Not-Knowing and the Therapist's Inner Conversation. *Family Process, 44*(4), 477–495. https://doi.org/10.1111/j.1545-5300.2005.00073.x

Rogers, M. E. (1970). *An introduction to the theoretical basis of nursing.* F. A. Davis.

Rosa, H. (2019). *Resonance: a sociology of our relationship to the world.* Polity.

Seikkula, J. (2008). Inner and outer voices in the present moment of family and network therapy. *Journal of Family Therapy, 30*(4), 478–491. https://doi.org/10.1111/j.1467-6427.2008.00439.x

Tønder, E. S., & Karlsson, B. E. (2020). Resonans i relasjoner (Resonance in relations). In N. Buus, B. Askham, & L. L. Berring (Eds.), *Psykiatrisk sykepleie* (pp. 375–398). Munksgaard. (Reprinted from 2nd.)

CHAPTER 9

A Map of Spiritual Literacy

> The longest and hardest journey humans will ever take is the short
> distance from the head to the heart.
> —*David Benner*

In the previous chapter, we looked more closely at the concept of literacy, and how we can link this, and give resonance, to spirituality. A key question is then: How to develop spiritual literacy in systemic family therapy practice? We will now, based on our study, present a theory in seven perspectives that can be a help in developing literacy, and create greater insight and understanding. We have called it "a map of spiritual and existential literacy" (See Fig. 9.1). The theory was developed through a PhD study where 15 family therapists and 12 clients were interviewed as part of the study. Constructive grounded theory was used as the research and analysis method. We will present the theory step by step and underpin it with reflections from therapists and clients. All quotes are from the PhD thesis (Holmberg 2018). Based on each perspective, there will be an activity for reflection. This can be done alone, in groups or in a teaching context. Our reflections make us better able to see where the shoe pinches, and what is needed to develop our spiritual path personally and professionally.

Å. Holmberg, P. Jensen, *Working with Spirituality in Family
Systemic Practice*, Palgrave Texts in Counselling and Psychotherapy,
https://doi.org/10.1007/978-3-031-77310-5_9

Fig. 9.1 "A map of spiritual and existential literacy"

RECOGNITION OF CLIENTS' SPIRITUAL AND RELIGIOUS EXPERIENCES, PRACTICE AND CULTURE

Recognition is a familiar but often difficult concept. It may be easy to say, but not always easy to perform in practice. Especially if there is something that we find difficult or that clashes with our values and faith or our philosophy of life.

How can clients know that you are acknowledging their spiritual life? Is it visible on the outside, or can they feel it? One way is to say initially that you hope to be open to all perspectives of life and include words such as spiritual, existential and religious. In our part of the world, many people are included by Christianity, and this has shaped their life journey, in both good and bad ways.

Recognition is an attitude, not a technique. The basic idea of recognition, re-cognize, is to "look again, to discern, fortify, acknowledge and strengthen" (Hegel 1977). In our context, it means focusing on and valuing the other person's inner world of experience (Schibbye 2009). It is a power of love, which we can find in relationships. By having an appreciative attitude, we help to build up the love that exists in the other (and ourselves). We can be touched by love. At certain moments we feel its presence. As therapists, we have to build up love and empathize with the other's subjective experience. Hegel says that this is only possible if an individual has access to his subjective world (Hegel 1977). Therefore, therapists have to ask: What does spirituality mean for me? Therapists with recognition create an atmosphere of security and can distinguish between their own and the other person's feelings and experiences. This cannot be underestimated; meeting a loving therapist can make all the difference. Like us, you have probably met therapists that you would never go to yourself. We must be the therapists people wish to meet.

Reflections about Practice
When I get new clients and they wonder who I am and what they can expect in therapy, I use to say that I want to be open to all aspects of life, physical, psychological, social, spiritual, cultural and religious. I have a thought that this could make it easier for people to talk about the spiritual and religious when it has already been stated. I often ask couples how they met each other, and if they say they met each other through church, I often ask what these perspectives mean for the couple today.

To relate to clients with love, we believe we need contact with the love in ourselves. This also involves distinguishing between our own experiences and those of our clients. It is not about remaking or forcing the other but making the other free—an inner recognition (Schibbye 2009). In love, life can be lived openly, in both thoughts and feelings. Recognition of clients' spiritual, existential or religious experiences, practice and culture is a prerequisite for spiritual and existential literacy. As therapists, we encounter a sea of differences concerning this topic, where everyone creates their own reality and has their own convictions. We have to face this openly and try to be with the other—where she or he is. One way to think about recognition is to have the mind and heart of a child, a beginner's mind. Children are open, honest and curious and do not have the barriers that we adults often have.

The concept of recognition comes from Hegel and has been further developed by Honneth (1995), who argues that we all have a moral responsibility to treat people with integration and recognition. He emphasizes that this is a universal duty and a virtue, developed from a consequential ethical perspective. For Honneth, recognition is about solidarity, promoting self-confidence, self-respect, and self-esteem, and protecting against violations.

Recognition can, in a therapeutic context, mean listening deeply and showing understanding, tolerance, acceptance and confirmation. Do not judge the other but tolerate the client's thoughts and feelings about spiritual matters. Be curious. To quote Kierkegaard: *In order to help another effectively, I must understand what he understands*, and accommodate the client's experiences. This requires an emotional presence, but also a continuous look at oneself as a therapist" (Schibbye 2009). We know that building a therapeutic relationship is essential for therapeutic work (Wampold and Imel 2015). In relation to spiritual issues, Gockel (2011) states that clients want therapists who can "tune in" with warmth, empathy, love, openness, acceptance and genuineness. If therapists are unable to respond to clients' spiritual needs, clients may experience distance (Post and Wade 2009). Recognition is about seeing clients' needs, reflections, feelings and wishes and giving them presence and space. The therapist will have a non-judgemental attitude that views the client's perspectives as most important. This presence and availability is a process that must be constantly kept alive.

Reflections from Therapists

Several of the therapists had reflections about the importance of recognition. Frode said:

> *I think acknowledging and accepting makes it possible for people to be present in their own lives. I think good onward paths for clients are about being able to be yourself, here and now; the best opportunities come from there.*

He wants all religions and views of life to have a place in his therapy room and said: "A professional approach to faith is being open; a mission is being closed". For example, he thinks that Christian therapists can help Muslims to stay safer with their faith.

Tomas, working in mental health, told a story about a young male client with drug and mental problems who once phoned him and asked him to pray "Our Father" with him. For a moment he hesitated, surely this was outside professional practice. But then he chose to accept the young man's wish. This therapist had recently become much more concerned with being open to clients' spiritual lives. He continued:

> Well, he called me. His great wish in life was to find security. He needed someone to have peace of mind with, and for me, it was his prayer more than mine. ... He asked me to do it [praying together]. ... He needed an anchor in life, and this was his only salvation. And I had to accept it. ... I had to be able to share it and, to some extent, participate in it.

Tomas was keen to meet all forms of expression of faith, saying:

> There is no faith that is better than others. There are different ways to relate to religions or systems of faith based on where you live and what culture you are a part of. Being a Muslim is just as "right" as being a Christian, a Buddhist, and even an atheist. A prerequisite for being able to talk about it is that there is no battle for truth or a fight for the right faith.

Nona, another therapist, was also concerned about recognition:

> I can grasp it, I can sort of recognize things they say, you know; I think they understand I'm a spiritual person, I think they understand, in the way I get responses ... you know, some are embarrassed talking about these things. And then I can say that I also believe in something more, you see. ... I feel it makes it easier for them to open up. ... I can say I believe in something more, so it's safe, you can talk about these things here.

Many therapists were interested in culture, and how culture affects our lives. Our own spiritual culture will affect us as therapists. One said:

> My experiences are based on stories from generations back in time. My data are stories told by my ancestors. I don't have a bachelor's degree in spirituality, it's not something I have read; it's experience-based stories.

Another had some similar ideas:

> *In a therapeutic context, I use my experiences from my own traditional culture, of experiences of living in a family of three generations. Of course, I include this when I talk to people, sometimes consciously and sometimes unconsciously. It's visible in therapeutic contexts, that's for sure.*

However, our cultural baggage can also make life closed and cramped. Edwin said:

> *I have a view of life that people should be free to live as they want to live and to be free from the morally charged norms and expectations that other people, other societies or cultures and systems of beliefs set up for people. Not without boundaries, understand me right, but within an ethical framework, which involves not abusing power and oppressing other people.*

Reflections from Clients

The clients were concerned about receiving recognition and found it crucial. One said:

> *I think it is fundamental to therapy. If you don't feel acknowledged, you have no benefit from being there. … The therapist must listen to what the client is saying and take that advice to heart.*

Recognition is acknowledging the "whole" human being.

One client, Tuva, said she had gone from shame and guilt to pride because of the recognition she had received from her current family therapist. She grew up in a very conservative Christian church, and her husband abused her mentally and physically. She felt embarrassed to have accepted this, but the therapist's acknowledgement did something to her. Showing her vulnerability, she compared her spiritual life to fragile greenhouse plants:

> *Religiosity is very sensitive or fragile, or how should I put it. It's deep in the soul. You must treat it with care. There are so many tough and strong opinions so it is almost like taking small greenhouse plants out in a strong wind, you know. … You have to keep them warm so they don't break … you can be assured that you won't be invaded by someone else's opinions, but you can let your statements stand like fragile plants.*

To sum up, recognition seems to give room for different kinds of spiritual life, as well as religious life. God can be important for clients, even without a particular religion. The important point seems to be whether there is room to talk about it or not. Clients want to be treated like whole beings. It also seems to be important not to downplay the client's religiosity, and to show curiosity, interest and acceptance. Spirituality may be a vulnerable topic, with both positive and negative experiences. It can be very concrete and about values and life choices, but also supernatural and transcendent. Clients may have experiences that may be difficult to understand—and to put into words. Couples and families may have value conflicts and cultural clashes, which can be explored together or separately.

Activity for Reflection

1. How do you recognize the spiritual clients?
2. How do you help clients to find freedom, inner peace and love?
3. Do you recognize your own spiritual life? In what way?
4. Do you have contact with love in your own life?

Working Systemically in Dialogue

We are all born into relationships, and thus into dialogue. Dialogue is an attitude, a way of relating to other people. We all have different views on life, but in a dialogue we have respect for the individual. We are not concerned with diagnosing the person. Hopefully, we have a view of people that embraces the whole person, an ecological perspective. The dialogue must be able to accommodate many voices, and we must be able to live with uncertainty and ambiguity. In a dialogue, we meet face to face and listen to each other. A dialogical discourse is open and inviting and encourages thinking together. The foreignness of the other makes dialogue possible. We can never fully understand each other. Each actor takes a position in the dialogical space. By changing our attitude and inviting the other to share feelings and actions, change can take place in the relationship.

To be systemic includes a spiritual focus. Systemic work is a way to meet the complexity of life, involving an ability to contemplate the whole. According to Telfener (2017), it is about seeing interconnections and patterns in a dynamic whole. We have to meet this complexity with curiosity and respect, to generate a multiverse where we also find ourselves as part of the whole. As therapists, we are responsible for our attitude, choices and use of language and need above all to have a reflective relationship with what we choose. Telfener states that human becoming is a result of biological, cultural, spiritual and psychological needs and is part of a construction of meaning. As therapists, we need to promote connection, have an attitude of curiosity, coexist with differences and be open to the unknown. As systemic therapists, we ask questions and listen to clients' stories. We must not forget the spiritual part of clients. This dimension may be incorporated into many other dimensions in their lives and may even be at the heart of conflicts and challenges.

Reflections from Supervision
In a group, students shared experiences about spirituality in practice. One student talked about a woman who had visited a shelter and said her husband was violent. Interestingly, her husband had sought out another shelter for men. In brief, it turned out that the stories of violence were made up because the couple were in a religious community where it was a sin to divorce. Violence (or adultery) was the only legitimate reason.
The therapists didn't know how to handle it.
Another student told of parents who distanced themselves from their teenage son and excluded him from the family. With further investigation, it emerged that this was done to try to force him to return to the family's religion. The boy was, according to their belief, on his way to hell, and this caused a lot of anxiety in the parents. The student could not remember how this was handled.
Both these stories are examples of where spiritual and religious factors are implicit in the narratives and could easily be overlooked if therapists do not include a spiritual focus. The stories also show that it can be a good idea to have knowledge of religious beliefs, as it can make therapists more confident in the dialogue, to find ways that can perhaps create new meaning together with the clients.

Larner (2017) argues that drawing on Bateson's systemic epistemology implies that we have to realize that every systemic conversation can evoke something of the spiritual. The question is whether therapists are open to it and listen for it. We have to look beyond the self and contemplate the "pattern which connects". Bateson and Bateson called it the sacred, a cybernetic spirituality based on humility and endless curiosity (Bateson and Bateson 1987). As systemic therapists, we are open to both/and thinking rather than either/or thinking and we create a dialogical room for different spiritual beliefs and theologies. We believe we have an ethical responsibility to relate to the client's spiritual life in an empathetic and loving way and not disregard clients' different perspectives on life.

Reflections from Therapists and Clients

In our study, both clients and therapists say that human spiritual life is intertwined with other perspectives in life. The human being is a system, connected to feelings and bodily experiences. It can be difficult to know which is which. One therapist, Frode, said:

> If people talk about faith, maybe they are talking about faith. But it can also be useful to see what they say from psychological perspectives. The opposite may also apply; when believers talk about life and psychology, it may be about faith, values and spirituality. ... I think to overlook certain forms of faith is unprofessional and shows a lack of interest and respect.

Nils, another therapist, was also keen to point out that different perspectives in people's lives influence each other:

> I think the soul, if that's what I should call it, is just as important as the body or the cognitive; it's all connected, and my experience in our Western society is that we still separate these things. The soul can be put aside, and we only talk about the rational, and the cognitive, ... we put aside the soul. In other cultures, it is more integrated and a bit more natural. I think it may be difficult for someone with psychological challenges if the soul is not part of the treatment.

Clients are part of different systems, such as a couple and family life, churches, mosques and different systems of faith. They may have a relationship with God and nature. Spirituality and religion can be important aspects of human culture.

Moving on to quotes by clients, Tone said that her spirituality infiltrated all spaces in her life:

> For me, it's quite big, it infiltrates everything, it infiltrates who I am as a person ... when I bring up my children, and meet people, it's a great part of my motivation ... for me, it's part of everything. It's a room where it's impossible to lock the door.

Maja felt that therapists must help clients to see how spiritual life affects life in general:

To make people aware of what they think, their opinions and thoughts about the big questions ... it's a value in itself. Hopefully, it will have positive effects on others, your partner, your children and others you meet. Becoming aware, that's part of developing as a human being. Yes, being more and more aware.

Systemic questions can help the therapist to connect with the spiritual life of clients. Further, genograms can provide insight into spiritual life through generations. Human beings are a system in themselves but are also part of many different systems where the spiritual has its place.

Activity for Reflection

1. In which ways do you include spirituality in your systemic therapeutic work for change?
2. How can you use your creativity to be more open-minded?
3. How do you deal with ethical challenges that you find objectionable?

Using Clients' Resources and Language

For many people, their spiritual life can be a great resource. Therefore, we think it makes no sense to obscure this dimension in therapy. It can support healing, connection and change. However, human spirituality can be both healthy and unhealthy, part of the problem or part of the solution, but by remaining silent, we cannot find out what this is like for the individual client. Our experience is also that it is much easier to downplay religion or spiritual experiences than to see opportunities and resources in them. An important focus in family therapy is to expand the family members' understanding of each other and to suggest new ways of being together. In the dialogue, we focus on resources, opportunities and cooperation in work for change. Regardless of the approach we use as therapists, questions about clients' spiritual lives can be linked up.

What kind of questions can help clients to come into contact with their spiritual life? Can phenomenological and religious words be of help? Words such as faith, mercy, hope, love, meaning and sacred? Religion has always needed the language of metaphors, symbols and stories. Symbolic language and metaphors can have the same ability as poetry to touch, bring together and lift. Metaphors have also been called poetry—in miniature. They are like symbols, creative and ambiguous. They go beyond language. Metaphors and symbols are also a kind of inner mirror, something to lean on when our feelings and experiences are very strong (Haram 2004). All languages are in a way metaphorical because a word is never the thing itself. It can only point to the thing. Knowing has to be balanced with not knowing.

Examples from Practice

A therapist said that she struggled with a couple who had major conflicts over their shared child (Holmberg 2012). She found them unreasonable, they could not collaborate, and they accused each other of one thing and another. At the end of the first session, she gave them a text from the Bible about the wise king Solomon that she wanted them to reflect on for the next time:

(1 King, 3: 16–24):

One day two women who were prostitutes came to Solomon. They stood before him. One of the women said, "My master, this woman and I live in the same house. I gave birth to a baby while she was there with me. Three days later this woman also gave birth to a baby. No one else was in the house with us. There were only the two of us. One night this woman rolled over on her baby, and it died. So during the night she took my son from my bed while I was asleep. She carried him to her bed. Then she put the dead baby in my bed. The next morning I got up to feed my baby. But I saw that he was dead! Then I looked at him more closely. I saw that he was not my son."

But the other woman said, "No! The living baby is my son. The dead baby is yours!"

But the first woman said, "No! The dead baby is yours, and the living one is mine!" So the two women argued before the king.

Then King Solomon said, "Each of you says the living baby is your own. And each of you says the dead baby belongs to the other woman."

Then King Solomon sent his servants to get a sword. When they brought it to him, he said, "Cut the living baby into two pieces. Give each woman half of the baby."

The real mother of the living child was full of love for her son. She said to the king, "Please, my master, don't kill him! Give the baby to her!"

But the other woman said, "Neither of us will have him. Cut him into two pieces!"

Then King Solomon said, "Give the baby to the first woman. Don't kill him. She is the real mother."

How can clients listen to the power in life? Frankl (2004) states that we all have an inner voice to guide us. Some call this source "God", while others call it "the true self" or "the still small voice". We can be led by dreams and fantasies, through creative impulses and desires that arise in our hearts and minds. Stepping into the unknown can provide unimaginable opportunities. How can people be free, let go of the past and live in the present?

Words are not always enough, especially when describing feelings. Then metaphorical language can be of great help, including stories, poems, music or pictures. A metaphor can help us to take a step back, and look at a situation "outside" ourselves. When words are not enough, a metaphor can open up the space in a new way. However, the use of metaphors is not suitable for everyone, and this is perhaps where therapeutic intuition comes in, what we call therapeutic wisdom. To dance the same dance.

Reflections from Therapists

The therapists said that being spiritual is part of being human. Human spirituality can have a healing effect and offer new openings for change. Spiritual sources can differ. In encounters with clients, therapists are concerned with ethics, values and meaning in life. The therapists described how spirituality was introduced into the narratives of clients or through the therapists' initiative. Nina said: "I want it to come naturally out of the things we are talking about and find out how they want to talk about these things". Not everyone wants to talk about spirituality. Tomas said that to find out you can ask: "This is important for many people, how is it for you?" In terms of language, Frode stated: "Professionalism is to grasp clients' belief systems, experiences and language universe". Language is power, and it is important to consider carefully the balance between the therapist and the client:

> *If you don't look critically at what you are saying, what you ask for in the conversation and what kind of words you use when talking to people, then you will be ... pushing people, even if you don't want to.*

Edwin felt that therapists must invite clients to find their own words, what is natural for them. The language of clients is the most effective door-opener. If necessary, therapists and clients can also fumble together.

Words can be explored. Language is full of values. Language often also includes metaphors which can be interesting and important to delve into further. Where do we find energy, something to connect to, some help to find a way forward?

The therapists also realized that religion could be an important perspective in the lives of clients. Edwin said that humans navigate their lives based on what they believe in. He felt that we inherently know what is good and what is not good in life, and that there are always values and a sense of meaning behind our actions. Values can be absent, but still implicit. He explained:

> *I think if people, if we all see that there is a relationship between the things we do and values that are deeply ingrained in us … then I think we'll live much better lives. I often think that when we're suffering, it's because there is disharmony between our practices, the actions we perform and the essential values that are part of us.*

Tomas also found talking about values to be very important. Sometimes values can be just a dream or a hope: "Questions and wondering about the meaning and interpretation of life become a journey, not an answer". Values bring people closer to their spiritual life. Suitable questions could be:

> *What do you hope for? What are your dreams? What kinds of values do you have? What do you think is good for you and your children? What kind of guidelines have you had from your childhood? What do you bring from home that you think is a strength and might give you balance in life?*

Several therapists felt that it was important not to overlook religious clients or clients for whom a relationship with God was important. Something deep emerges in people when they are at the outer limits of their existence, on the verge of a mental or physical breakdown. Frode found that clients with great faith seemed to handle pain in a better way. They can see possibilities in the darkness. He said: "I relate to faith because it gives access to resources like friends in 'higher places' … and, for some, truths to keep them going in the middle of the storm". He continued:

> *Believing in ghosts is more accepted than believing in God; it would be best if clients come to someone who opens up … doesn't think they're 'mad'. That's something we should look at and take seriously.*

Maybe psychology and Darwin explain faith in crises as the kind of idea that provides the best survival in a godless random world. Maybe it's the opposite, that life and the eternity of realities become clear in these situations. … We are ultimately not only dependent on love in relationships in this ephemeral life but on the great drama in the eternal; it is only God who can help.

Therapists ask clients how they talk to God and how they think God can help. God can give comfort and a feeling that they are not alone. Which aspect of your faith is helpful for you? Some use a whiteboard, where God can be drawn, as a figure, a symbol or a name. It can be a relief to talk about God in therapy.

Frode said that people's constructions of God, or their learned constructions, can be problematic in life and affect people in different ways. Exploring this can be a way to find new solutions to challenges. He told a story where his client talked more about Jesus than herself. He found that this blocked and obscured other challenges. To clarify this, he wondered whether Jesus could move out into the waiting room during the conversation. The client said yes, and Frode then opened the door, and closed it again, to make this clear. He also recalled having met believers who used strong religious language, and said they heard God's voice, but upon closer examination, it all fell apart. He felt that as therapists we must be on the lookout for a belief that is unhealthy for life and relationships.

REFLECTIONS FROM CLIENTS

One client, John, said that Norwegians were very shy about mentioning spiritual perspectives, especially religion. He felt that people needed to develop their language and may be *simply out of tune.*

Help can be found in metaphors, such as "faith like an anchor" or "the voice of the heart". Maja explained that her spiritual life was nourished through films, pictures, poems, novels, songs and music, and said that the way the therapist talks is crucial for her:

Having an open voice, wondering, someone who insists that the invisible, spiritual and religious values exist, and who knows this is crucial for couples to develop as human beings.

She found it important for a couple to explore what gives power, spirit and unity. She believed that the therapist needed to be proactive in questioning, friendly and wondering, and someone who could also develop the differences in the couple. Especially regarding spiritual needs.

Lisbeth said that clients need help and support to explore how their spirituality can help them:

I think if you go deep inside yourself, you can know the power, which is God in one way, and much bigger than you yourself. And it has carried me through all those years of violence and all that. And it also gave the children strength.

Many of the clients said that leaning on God was a decisive and important factor in their lives. Stian described this as follows:

Life has some ups and downs. When you get your downs and have nothing to hold you up, to use that kind of expression, I think not having something outside myself, only trusting entirely my own existence, no, that wouldn't work out, it wouldn't work out.

Bjørn had similar experiences:

I just said to God, 'Right, you need to help me get through this. I don't think I can handle it alone.' This is a great strength and I think that's the point of Christianity. I think many people's experience is that Christianity is about following rules and you have to live life in a special way; but for me, it's been the opposite. I'm not so good at following the rules and living right and properly, but forgiveness and support from God are with me all the time.

Several of the informants said that their relationship with God was the main reason why they were alive today.

Activity for Reflection

---

1. What are your spiritual resources?
2. Are you comfortable talking about your spiritual life with others? If not, what do you think is the reason?
3. How do you find spiritual resources in clients?
4. Can God be part of your therapy? In what ways?
5. What kind of spiritual language feels natural to you? When do you feel resistance?

BRIDGING LINGUISTIC UNCERTAINTY

Sinclair and Chochinov (2012) say that language may be the greatest barrier to talking about spirituality in therapy. There are many definitions of spirituality, existentiality or religion, and therapists may feel unsure about what words to use. In addition, spirituality is not always so easy to put into words, at least not its transcendent aspects. However, the Benedictine monk Christopher Jamison (2022) says the problem of today is the loss of a spiritual language. He believes we are losing the ability to talk about love and joy, kindness, hatred and greed, to name a few topics. Jamison calls this "the transcendent". He says that language in the West today is a practical business language, where the aim is to sell or convince us of something or give us more technical insight. Language is not just a communication tool; it makes us human. If we have been greeted with kind words that touch the heart, we can remember it with gratitude. Careless or harsh words can leave lasting wounds. How we speak matters.

How can we develop and become more spiritually sensitive? First and foremost, it is about paying attention to our spiritual life. If this is completely foreign to us, we will most likely find it difficult to translate the topic into language in therapy. The next step is to throw ourselves into deep water—and start swimming. To acquire competence will always be a work in progress. The clinical psychologist Philip Brownell (2015) argues that including spirituality is a blind spot in psychotherapy training, but that through knowledge, practice and experience, we will be on safer ground.

Reflections from Therapists and Clients

Many of the therapists admitted that they lacked language in encounters with a client's spiritual life. The reasons were the silence in the field and in family therapy education or a lack of interest or uncertainty about how to approach this area. Tor, an atheist, said, "I don't even think about asking the question". However, he saw that there could be strengths and opportunities he might have overlooked. Another therapist felt that she had been far too sensitive, but "How do I talk about it?" It has become a habit not to include the topic. For many, it is a taboo.

Lisbeth, a client, thought that therapists were afraid and said they had to be "faith-neutral":

> *Perhaps they're afraid to offend anyone. You think that you should not step into someone's space when it comes to religion. At the same time, it's a very big part of everyday life for many people, and I think a lot more ... than you might think.*

Lisbeth went on to say that her much-loved therapist seemed unsure about going into spiritual topics, and the therapist had to make sure that this was on her own terms. She recalled that the therapist said:

> *This is not within the approved context of family counselling, but you are a spiritual person, and so am I, so we agree, you know, that this is an important issue in your life. That's why we talk about it, isn't it?*

Henrik, for his part, felt that including spirituality conflicted with being professional and believed that therapists are afraid of their colleagues. He had experience in child and adolescent psychiatry and thought that God and religion could be of great help. But this aspect was absent:

> *It was pure psychiatry, observations and a large resource team. ... Nothing spiritual they could lean on. It was cognitive "pegs": awareness of their strengths.*

Maja had had similar experiences:

> *I miss the questions, you see? Questions like, what is your faith? Or, what do you believe in...? Do you talk about these things? What does it mean to you ... in your relationship? Both practically and theoretically ... in their hearts, in a way.*

Several of the clients thought that therapists were "out of tune" and needed to develop their language skills.

Activity for Reflection

---

1. Look at the "spirituality box" below. Which words are natural to use for you—and why?Do you have other words?
   Spirituality
   View of life
   Philosophy of life
   Faith
   Values
   Promise
   Existential themes
   Understanding of reality
   Meaning of life
   Soul
   The sacred
   Religion
   The transcendent
   The mysterious
   Metaphysical
2. What kind of words do you use in sessions with clients?
3. How can you develop your spiritual language?
4. What kind of "language" do you have available in your practice?

INCREASING PERSONAL AWARENESS AND COMPETENCE

We all need to stop now and then and reflect on who we are, what we hope for and what we think is the meaning of life. To live as authentically as possible is to live where our heart is. Knowing ourselves is important for working as a therapist. It is therefore also important to be aware of our own spirituality and our own spiritual journey. This also applies to psychological aspects. As therapists, we need to be aware of our own feelings, our emotional experience in life. We all have our vulnerable points. As therapists we need to work on our life themes, so that they are included in therapy. We ourselves must grow and be in development. In the therapeutic relationship, we need to be emotionally open. We need to be firmly grounded, able to take a risk and relate to the client from an inside perspective.

It is easy to overlook or override parts of conversations if we find the topics difficult or not worth reflecting on. Everything we see is shaped by our knowledge, experience and culture. If we dare to be honest about our spiritual life, we will find our own biases that we need to work on. However, this should also be a pleasant undertaking. We believe our spiritual life is an enrichment, a powerful source of meaning, joy and hope. Life moves fast, and it is too short to sleepwalk through it. Our spiritual senses can often be dormant. We therefore think we need to reflect on our spiritual journey.

One perspective that we should be extra observant about is our relationship with religion. The clients in our study found that therapists could talk about meaning and values, but this was not linked to their religious life. It appears to be a vulnerable topic, and as therapists we should also be able to accept children's religious language. As one of our informants said:

If it's part of the client's, or the patient's, or the family's narratives, if it's something important to them, then the therapist must give this room ... and not be afraid of it. ... If it's important to that person, the therapist must face it and be open and willing to go deeper.

Gergen (2009) says that this is also something educational institutions should address:

It is not enough for the scholarly community to smugly view religious traditions as havens of mythology. If scholarly work is to make a significant contribution to the culture that sustains it, open dialogue is imperative. Failing to take up such dialogue is to establish yet another island of practice, separated from others by an ocean of alienation. (p. 352)

Therefore, we believe we have to reflect on the theoretical and philosophical basis on which we build our practice. We think we should also be open to drawing in other perspectives, such as humanistic psychology or existential psychotherapy. We feel the need to delve more into the individual, and how this affects the relational aspect. If we are only concerned with what is in between, we can easily lose the spiritual client. The therapist's knowledge, sensitivity and awareness of spirituality will influence the dialogical process. The therapist's language has to be in harmony with the language of the client.

Reflections from Therapists

Several of the therapists stated that reflecting on their own spiritual journey made them more open and sensitive. Tomas is one of them. During his spiritual journey, he felt he could sense clients' spirituality better than before:

From being a believer to perhaps becoming a non-believer, to be doubtful, to acknowledge in my own life that there is a question that always will be there, and never resolved ... and ... and have a deeper sound than I realized. Then I think it ... it makes me better at sensing it now.

Tomas thought that Muslim clients had reminded him, because of their openness about faith:

Without me asking directly, nearly all of them say that God or Allah is an important guide in life. God holds a protective hand over them. Many adhere to the concept of "inshallah", meaning "if God wants"; there is a lot of fate-oriented thinking among them, but still, when they talk about escape, crises, war, I notice that God or Allah has an important function in their lives: God is a helper or a protector, a way to handle adversity and pain.

Tomas was going to retire soon, and now he did what he wanted, which he felt was good for the client. He said, "I'm not afraid of using myself any more", and he thought resonance was necessary. Resonance can provide golden moments in therapy.

Kari acknowledged that it was her own obstacles that blocked spirituality in therapy: "I think, if you can break the barrier with yourself because it is often about yourself, then I think that will give the client much greater security". She thus hoped that greater awareness would enable her to explore the spirituality of clients more naturally.

Knowing about different religious practices and beliefs was highlighted as an important aspect. Ada, herself an atheist, invited a Buddhist couple to share what faith meant to them. What she discovered was that belief became a block in the relationship, blocking growth and development:

His view was 'I must be good, I have to accept things, accept things, accept things.' And this was their source of trouble. Because just by accepting, nothing could be done for them, so it was an example of something that creates their challenges. ... And then they became violent, do you understand what I mean? They got very aggressive with each other, which is not close to Buddhism ... as you know; it was quite challenging to work and to use this to help them therapeutically because their faith in itself was a block.

Nevertheless, Ada tried to be respectful and analytical, and draw other perspectives into their lives to develop their spiritual universe.

Supernatural Experiences
Our experience is there is more between heaven and earth. Sometimes we
have experiences that we do not fully understand or that we can call supernatural. The therapists talked about clients' spiritual experiences, which
affected them physically, psychologically and relationally. These experiences could be both positive and negative. One example was contact with
deceased family members. A therapist told of a young man admitted to
psychiatric care who said that he could hear, see and smell his dead father.
There were different opinions in the professional team as to whether he
needed more medicine or whether they should try to go more deeply into
his story. The family therapist pointed out that there may have been a difficult father-son relationship. The therapist began to explore the client's
childhood, and it turned out that when the boy was small his father had
abused him. As the son grew bigger and stronger, he began to mistreat his
father. Now he was convinced that his father had returned to take revenge
and give him no peace. The young man found that talking to the therapist
made his father and the experiences much less prominent: "We were suddenly speaking the same language. This relationship became the basis for
the dialogue, and the father's activities in the house disappeared more
and more".

Frode recalled a mother who spoke to her dead daughter. He was keen
to acknowledge the experiences, the feelings and the context. The mother
was in deep grief, and the therapist wanted to talk calmly and slowly about
this. The therapists Frode asked what she hoped for her daughter after
death, and what she thought was important to pass on from her daughter
to her children. He asked the mother to write a letter to her daughter,
organized a sermon at the grave, and invited the mother's network in for
dialogue. He said:

> *In that way, one takes both perspectives seriously—both the revenant as spiritual*
> ***and*** *the grief, shock and trauma as psychological. At the same time, I have to*
> *relate to the fact that there may be neither one nor … it could be anything …*
> *forgiveness, acknowledgement, security, belonging, and above all … what I*
> *have never come across or had thoughts about.*

Frode was interested in the idea that spirituality and psychology could
be two sides of the same issue:

> *"Is this psychology or spirituality? For therapists, it can be useful to think it's*
> *both or either. I aim to help psychologically, spiritually and relationally".* He

also believed that the spiritual can be implicit when clients talk in terms of psychological perspectives.

Spiritual Practice
The therapists felt that it could be important to include spiritual practice. This could be scripture, praying, rituals, mindfulness and even astrology. Frode said:

> *In serious moments, biblical texts are useful, especially for people who are not Christians. For them, the texts are not a compulsion. Often, I think they perceive them as fables, anecdotes or good perspectives that connect them to major concepts like life, the time of a generation, context, hope, forgiveness, reconciliation and peace.*

Rituals can help clients to move on in life. Regarding prayer, the therapists were divided, but Nina said she can pray if that is what clients want:

> *It is a need for God, a spiritual connection and a need for the power of God. I think this is common to every religion, and that's why I could pray with clients, whatever religion they may have.*

Becoming aware of one's breathing is also a way to calm down and get closer to one's spirituality. Clients may be stressed and anxious, but helping clients to breathe calmly can be a way to get in touch with their inner life. One way can be:

> *Find a calm breathing pattern. Allow the inhalation to expand, as if you were breathing into a large room. Every time you breathe in, imagine that everything you need is drawn into your body, energy, power and vitamins—only your imagination sets the limits. When you breathe out, imagine letting go of everything you don't need, letting it flow out and being washed out of your body and mind.* (Myskja 2015, p. 25)

REFLECTIONS FROM CLIENTS

Several of the clients said that therapists need knowledge about spirituality and religion. Clients must be able to ask relevant questions and address the topic safely and openly:

I think it certainly is important to clarify for therapists. Yes, like we talked about in the beginning, spirituality and faith and so on are so private. But maybe they have a job to do, to be exposed to them. So that you know where you stand and are confident yourself before you can ... go into someone else's problems. And it's also about knowing what kind of understanding you have. So you know your view on the matter, which you must try not to transfer to others because you must be available for the person you will help.

Knowing that therapists have "inside" information made it easier to be open about faith and church life:

It was lovely to be able to be a bit sarcastic, where I could sort of make fun of the experiences of the church. I could do it because I felt we had something in common, in some way a similar background.

Many of the clients also said that they wanted to know something about the spirituality of the therapists. It would make the therapeutic room safer. However, there must also be openness to different religions and worldviews. Some even felt that if therapists were unable to go into this topic, then they should know other therapists they can refer to. Tona said:

If a therapist feels spiritual issues are difficult to talk about, I think it's better if the therapist suggests another therapist, because they know someone else who can handle it well. If a doctor didn't know enough about joints, he'd recommend an orthopaedic surgeon.

This was supported by Anette, who said:

For me and many others, faith is the most important thing, so if the therapy clashes with your main ideas, then the therapy will kind of fall flat. If you get a match [with the therapist], it will be much more solid.

However, it is not a simple matter to ask for a new therapist. Clients are generally polite and do not want to embarrass the therapists.

Activity for Reflection

---

1. How can you grow and develop on a deeper level?
2. Start spending 15 minutes in silence every day. Sit down, light a candle and breathe calmly, or go for a walk in nature, without music in your ears. Buy a nice notebook and note down the reflections that come to you.
3. Reflect on your relationship with religion. What did you grow up with? What have you discarded—and what have you taken with you into adult life? What kind of relationship do you have with other religions? How can you be more open to religion in your practice?

WORKING WITH PERSONAL OBSTACLES

If we sense an uneasiness in relation to spiritual and religious reflections, it can be difficult to be dialogical. We can easily resort to strategic solutions to regain control. The dialogical space narrows when we focus more on giving advice to others. It becomes difficult to hear different voices. The road easily gets to be too narrow.

There is much that can block spiritual life, especially stress and everything else that we fill our lives with. Based on our understanding, a lack of spiritual contact will lead to a void within us that must be filled. Vetere says (2023) that we cannot find peace in restlessness; we need time to pause, to reflect and think over our lives. What is the danger? What are my obstacles? The body and our emotions can show the way, such as our breathing, heart rate and muscle tension. When we feel physical resistance to a topic, we can try to explore what our body is trying to tell us.

Listening to the Body

We believe that listening to the body often can be underestimated. How often do we ask clients about what the body says? Can we help clients to let the body tell?

One way is to sit relaxed, close your eyes and breathe calmly. Then you can encourage the client to feel whether there are tensions or imbalances in the body. Here you can first feel it on the left side, then the right. Is there a difference between the parts? Is there an imbalance? Encourage clients to pay full body attention. What do you notice? What sensory experiences and images emerge? What thoughts and feelings come up?

Once you have given this some time, the clients can share what they want to share.

(Myskja 2015)

Reflections from Therapists

Despite the importance of the topic and the fact that several therapists included spirituality in silence, they still had considerable resistance to the topic. They had obstacles, such as a lack of interest, feeling embarrassed or unreflective on the topic, believing that it is too private, feeling uncertain, having no time, having no experience and feeling that it was not politically correct, to mention a few barriers. Nils called it "a scary little black hole" and said that excluding spirituality can be a habit because of the feeling of taboo.

Tor had worked as a therapist for several decades and did not believe in God or anything supernatural. The spiritual universe had no connotation for him. However, he saw therapy as "a liberating unification with new experience and opportunities for action", but still left out the spirituality of the client. He said: "I cannot see any point in asking whether people believe in God. But if they refer to it, I'm not sure what to do about it". Like Tor, several other therapists were unsure of how to talk about the topic and the purpose of including it.

For Terje, to include God was out of the question. Åse asked him:

> I: *If we're thinking systemically, if someone has a relationship with God, can God be part of the therapy? If you have an empty chair, can God "sit there"? What would God say?*
>
> T: *Yes, but I don't think we could bring him in here … I think that's is a job for the priest or a psychologist or something like that.*

When you meet others with different beliefs or values from you own, dialogue can be difficult. Tomas said that in his struggle with the church and religious dogma, he could easily get into similar conflicts. He also found it difficult if clients are fundamentalist in their beliefs, as that triggers his frustrations. Then there may be a risk that clients do not feel recognized. Grete had similar reflections, saying that it must be difficult to enter the spiritual world of clients if you do not believe in it yourself:

> *Just how easy is it to sit there and talk about the spiritual … at least the Christian spiritual dimension, in the therapy context, if you don't have any relationship to it …? Maybe you should say, if someone says they would like to talk about it, maybe they should change their therapist?*

REFLECTIONS FROM CLIENTS

The clients had a great deal of advice and reflections on how therapists should act concerning this topic. We have already mentioned several perspectives, but they emphasized that they wanted therapists who could include spirituality and religious issues and were transparent about their own life. Maja said:

> *Having an open voice, wondering, someone who insists that the invisible, spiritual and religious values exist, and who knows this is crucial for couples to develop as human beings.*

Lisbet felt that it made a world of difference if she could nourish the spiritual dimension. Everything is connected to everything.

One man said that if therapists fail to include their clients' spiritual lives, they have a real handicap. He believes that therapists must reawaken their spiritual space to be professional. Therapists also need to know that the spiritual aspect can be a source of emotional distance in a couple's relationship. Eva and Jon, for example, come from two very different religious traditions. She is from a more dogmatic, conservative tradition, and he is from a more open, liberal context. This has been difficult for their relationship, especially in bringing up their children. They both think it would be useful if their differences could be reflected on with a therapist. Henrik also had something to say about this. He is a Christian, but his wife is an atheist. He said: "Just ask about it. Find out about different faiths. … Someone could help me to talk about what I might find difficult to talk about by myself". In therapy, family members can learn to listen to each other, helping respect and tolerance to grow and giving space to the differences.

Activity for Reflection

---

1. Sit quietly for some minutes and ask yourself: What are your obstacles to including spirituality in therapy? Listen to your feelings, thoughts and bodily reactions. If there are several of you together, share what you are experiencing.
2. How do you think these obstacles have arisen?
3. How can you overcome your obstacles?
4. Who can help you to overcome them?
5. The combination of the emotional and the spiritual can be difficult to deal with. How can you handle it in your practice?

BREAKING THE SILENCE IN THE PUBLIC SPACE

When we started collaborating on this PhD project ten years ago, there was little talk about the topic. Åse remembers that Per said, "You're just a bit early", and we believe his vision was correct. But now something is going on! We find that both colleagues and students are interested, the topic is now more often raised in the public space. However, things are not moving very fast, and we would like help from more people who want to highlight this perspective. There is a need for more research and development. In addition, in the same way that we need spiritual literacy, we also think we need critical literacy. Here the focus is on marginal voices and reflecting critically on dominant discourses and ideologies in a field (Luke 2012). Systemic family therapy is a field in motion. It has been since the beginning. We all have a responsibility to lift up marginalized voices, and work to free ourselves from habits that are oppressive and constraining (Freire 1979). We need activities to work on ourselves, or clients will show us up. What we say and do, how we present ourselves physically and relationally, all reveal something about us. Silence also has a language. It tells people about our spirituality, implicitly and explicitly. The former clinical associate professor Harry Aponte (2009) says:

All therapy rests on a spiritual platform of values and a philosophical outlook that reflects the spirituality of clients and the clinician's therapeutic philosophy. (p. 130)

Aponte believes that therapists are often unaware of how spirituality affects their practice. Through critical reflection, we can develop ourselves as therapists and the field in general.

A good example of a meeting between different therapy cultures and reflections about spirituality was a collaboration between the Family Centre, the Dulwich Centre and indigenous Maori therapists from New Zealand (Waldegrave 2003). They found that together they had a big problem in relation to spirituality. The European therapists worked in a secular tradition, where body and soul were separate parts. For the Maori, body and soul were interconnected, and it was impossible to think about healing without spirituality being a natural part. They therefore tried together to find a path that they could all feel comfortable with. They concluded that spirituality is essentially about relationships from four perspectives. First, there is a relationship between people and the natural environment, such as mountains, the sea and clouds. The next point was that being spiritual was about justice and kindness between people. All forms of goodness and acts of beauty are acts of the sacred. The third perspective was about cultural belongings, ancestry, and honouring people's heritage. There can be many difficult stories that are propagated in shame, but through new stories linked to identity and belonging, new success stories can emerge in the present. The fourth and final perspective on spirituality was about people and the numinous. This was the transcendence, the world beyond, or what some call God. After reaching this common platform, it felt great to write a poem, music, or a story from nature, and it created a common new language. Therapy was called sacred exchange, a spirit of liberation, facilitating new and transformed meaning with the goal of hope and reconciliation. A notion of sacredness became the participants' primary metaphor for therapy.

Reflections from Therapists

Almost all the therapists in our study said that spirituality and religion were under-communicated in the family therapy field. They felt that spirituality had no obvious place in the Western therapeutic culture. It was not a topic discussed among colleagues, nor in education, nor in journals or conferences. Some even said it was difficult to include spirituality in systemic methods. A large interpretative frame of life was seldom part of the sessions. However, clients' values could often be included, but not explored in a deeper way by looking into the client's spiritual life or spiritual needs.

Tomas told us that his experience stretched back to the 60s when he was young and newly graduated. Psychologists and social workers revolted against authority, and Christianity and religion in general were seen as oppressive. He believes that the revolt was necessary, even if it was probably more about protest about dogmas and religious practices than against God and faith itself. Today, he believes that the pendulum has swung back. The old divide between the religious and the material is less visible, and people seek spirituality more on their own paths.

Another therapist, Kari, said that she works with a Christian therapist who has never invited clients to share anything from their spiritual life. She said the following about the therapist:

She listens to the morning prayer on the radio every morning, reads the Bible
and other Christian texts and so on, but still, when we work together, this is
never a topic of conversation. It's just between us privately. That's strange.

The therapy group in our study told us that, in their practice, they
incorporate folk beliefs and various religions to a much greater extent. In
the systemic family therapy field in general, they have felt a lack of recognition when they wanted to include spirituality:

Usually, when we come up with such interpretations, we are seen as a little
exotic, sometimes perhaps that we're not quite normal. Some think this is non-
sense and, especially, many regard it as not professional.

However, what is interesting is that even if the therapists did not talk to
colleagues about spirituality, or bring up the topic when giving advice,
many still included it in their practice, in silence.

REFLECTIONS FROM CLIENTS

The clients in our study said that they had the feeling that spirituality does
not quite fit into family therapy. Religion was even worse, a disturbing element, and too private for therapy. Some felt that therapists were afraid to
offend people or worried about what their colleagues might think of them.
Others said that therapists were not allowed to include spirituality; it is not
part of the professional work. They thought that therapists had not learned
to include the topic and that they could not handle it.

Activity for Reflection

---

1. We see a different openness towards spiritual matters, in society, among colleagues
   and students, then we saw a few years ago. What is your experience?
2. How can you break the silence in a public space?
3. What do you think the systemic therapeutic field needs in order to include spiritual,
   existential and religious perspectives to a greater extent?

REFERENCES

Aponte, H. J. (2009). The stress of povertry and the comfort of spirituality. In F. Walsh (Ed.), *Spiritual resources in family therapy* (2 ed., pp. 125–140). The Guliford Press.

Bateson, G., & Bateson, M. C. (1987). *Angels fear: towards an epistemology of the sacred.* Macmillan.

Brownell, P. (2015). *Spiritual competency in psychotherapy* (1st ed.). Springer Publishing Company.

Frankl, V. E. (2004). *Man's search for meaning: the classic tribute to hope from the Holocaust.* Rider.

Freire, P. (1979). *Pedagogy of the oppressed.* Sheed and Ward.

Gergen, K. J. (2009). *Relational being: beyond self and community.* Oxford University Press.

Gockel, A. (2011). Client Perspectives on Spirituality in the Therapeutic Relationship [Article]. *Humanistic Psychologist, 39*(2), 154–168. https://doi.org/10.1080/08873267.2011.564959

Haram, A. (2004). *Dialogens kraft: når tanker blir stemmer (The power of dialogue. When thoughts become voices.).* Universitetsforl.

Hegel, G. W. (1977). *Phenomenology of spirit.* Oxford University Press.

Holmberg, Å. (2012). Familieterapeuters møte med det åndelige og eksistensielle mennesket. *Fokus på familien, 40*(01), 49–66.

Holmberg, Å. (2018). *Making room for spirituality?: family therapists' and clients' perceptions and experiences about spirituality in family therapy* VID Specialized University]. Oslo.

Honneth, A. (1995). *The struggle for recognition: the moral grammar of social conflicts.* Polity Press.

Jamison, C. (2022). *Finding the language of grace.* Bloomsbury Publishing Plc.

Larner, G. (2017). Spiritual Dialogues in Family Therapy. *Australian and New Zealand Journal of Family Therapy, 38*(1), 125–141. https://doi.org/10.1002/anzf.1207

Luke, A. (2012). Critical literacy: Foundational notes. *Theory into practice, 51*(1), 4–11.

Myskja, A. (2015). *Helbred deg selv: styrk din egen motstandskraft* (p. 213). Klim.

Post, B. C., & Wade, N. G. (2009). Religion and spirituality in psychotherapy: a practice-friendly review of research [Article]. *Journal of Clinical Psychology, 65*(2), 131–146. http://search.ebscohost.com/login.aspx?direct=true&db=afh&AN=36078396&site=ehost-live

Schibbye, A.-L. L. (2009). *Relasjoner: et dialektisk perspektiv på eksistensiell og psykodynamisk psykoterapi* (2. utg. ed.). Universitetsforl.

Sinclair, S., & Chochinov, H. M. (2012). Communicating with patients about existential and spiritual issues: SACR-D work. *Progress in Palliative Care*, *20*(2), 72–78. https://doi.org/10.1179/1743291X12Y.0000000015

Telfener, U. (2017). Becoming through Belonging: The Spiritual Dimension in Psychotherapy. *Australian and New Zealand Journal of Family Therapy*, *38*(1), 156–167. https://doi.org/10.1002/anzf.1199

Vetere, A. (2023). We cannot find peace in restlessness. How the neuroscience supports psychotherapeutic practice. *Human Systems*, 26344041231203378.

Waldegrave, C. (2003). Grappling with a contemporary and inclusive spirituality. *Just Therapy–a Journey: A Collection of Papers from the Just Therapy Team* New Zealand Adelaide: Dulwich Centre Publications.

Wampold, B. E., & Imel, Z. E. (2015). *The great psychotherapy debate; The Evidence for What Makes Psychotherapy Work*. Routledge.

CHAPTER 10

Concluding Remarks

May you be a peace.
May your heart remain open.
May you awake to the light
of your own true nature.
May you be healed.
May you be a source of healing for all beings.
—Tibetan Buddhist Prayer

Part I in this book introduced the concept of spirituality as one possible framework for systemic family therapy. It started by introducing spirituality as an important part of clinical practice, with a systemic view on spirituality. The clients will always be in the centre in this practice.

We moved on to present spirituality as a multifaceted landscape. The concept is used in both religious and non-religious contexts. It is used in many different religious and spiritual communities and in secular communities (humanistic spirituality). We presented spiritual sources in human life and how spirituality might even have a toxic element.

We looked briefly at the history of spirituality and psychotherapy and in more detail at spirituality in systemic family therapy. We also presented some tools for including spirituality in family therapy.

© The Author(s), under exclusive license to Springer Nature   167
Switzerland AG 2024
Å. Holmberg, P. Jensen, *Working with Spirituality in Family
Systemic Practice*, Palgrave Texts in Counselling and Psychotherapy,
https://doi.org/10.1007/978-3-031-77310-5_10

Today most of us live in multicultural societies. One chapter is about spirituality in intercultural family therapy. Here we present what might happen when west meets east and when collectivism meets individualism. We discuss what happens when spirituality in different family cultures meets the therapist's own spirituality and what happens when the professional's culture meets the client's culture.

Another chapter concerns obstacles to including spirituality in therapy. It is about "the big silence" and the lack of language to talk about spirituality in systemic family therapy. Many clients and therapists are used to excluding spirituality from professional conversations and that might be one explanation for why it is silenced.

Part II is about making room for spirituality. We present existential psychotherapy and existential health. Then we move on to how to develop spiritual literacy in dialogical practice. Here we present the concept of literacy and how to use it in systemic family therapy. We introduce the concept of resonance and how it interacts between the therapist and the client or family.

In Chap. 9 we present a map of spiritual literacy. In addition to the presentation of the map, we invite readers to complete several assignments and to reflect around spirituality and systemic family therapy.

This book is by no means complete. Hopefully, more people will join us, through research, theory development and further reflections. There is a need for research in relation to children, young people, different practice contexts, mental health and the inclusion of spirituality in different theoretical approaches, to name a few. There is a need for clinicians who discuss this topic with their colleagues and together link the perspectives into their practice. There is also a need to develop different teaching programmes linked to the topic. Further, the book is an invitation to you, the reader: How can you relate to this?

New voices emphasize the need for an expanded view of humanity in treatment, we need a "both-and" attitude, where the spiritual and existential aspects of man are highlighted. Even if existential challenges manifest themselves physically and socially, this does not have to be an illness. We must search deeper and wider. People's relational challenges also have an existential perspective. In today's society, psychological pain, discomfort and difficult relationships are often given diagnostic categories, while the language we use to describe life is inadequate. Spiritual and existential literacy open up for a language that includes our whole life, and the question is how to make letters for this alphabet. It must be a language that intertwines body, soul and spiritual and existential perspectives. Here, sensitivity and awareness are important perspectives, helping us to be able to "read" a situation (Arman et al. 2013). All therapists have a base of values, beliefs, morals and a view of humanity that forms the basis for a meaning in life. With this as a basis, together with our theoretical and methodological approaches, we will help clients find a path that makes sense for the individual.

The existential therapist Irvin Yalom (2015) says that the most important thing therapists can do is to offer an authentic healing relationship, where the client can take in what gives meaning on the life path. He believes that we must help clients to see their lives in a far wider context than the therapy room. Yalom explains that we may never know exactly how we were helpful, but we must learn to live with that mystery as we follow the client's journey. He urges us not to lose sight of the whole person. He says that many existential challenges are hidden behind what he calls "traditional categories". Yalom believes that far more people than we think struggle with existential questions and challenges. He feels that therapists must have much greater sensitivity to these perspectives in people's lives.

Maybe we have to dare a little more? Do not be so politically correct in all situations: doing what we think others think is right, and ignoring our own reflections and feelings. This is strictly speaking no big risk. It is probably much worse if clients have to withhold important life-giving resources in therapy. We think it is a human right to have a space where spiritual, existential and religious perspectives can also have a place. If existential health can be strengthened, it can be an important asset in the big picture.

DEVELOPING YOUR PRACTICE

Human beings are human becomings. When troubles arrive, how can spirituality help us to get back into the flow of things and expand our consciousness and identity? We want to help people be more whole; being is never static, we are always on the move. The glasses you wear will shape your world.

In this book, we have highlighted the theory of "a map of spiritual and existential literacy", and we hope you have been encouraged and inspired to include spiritual perspectives in your practice.

Therapists can help clients to see new possibilities that they did not see before. However, sometimes these just confirm something you already knew. A person may just need a little more power and strength to go that way. The Norwegian psychologist Annbjørg Haram (2004) describes how hope can gradually emerge, like the sun waiting behind the clouds. We need dreams, visions and hope. Without this, our creativity and vitality can disappear. The dialogue and the relationship are key elements in a therapeutic setting.

As we have shown in this book, spirituality can be a source of strength, connection, meaning and new creativity. As Telfener (2017) argues:

> *Spirituality is not something concrete we can buy on the market, it is not a commodity that we can or cannot possess. It is a drive that emerges from the questions that concern the living and can become an everyday practice that brings an expansion to our awareness, creating a virtuous cycle that self-enhances itself. It is a connection that connects us to the universal being, an attitude embodied in inter-subjectivity that forces us to abandon our certainties and our thirst for order.* (Telfener 2017)

This power is a source that everyone has access to and can become more aware of. As therapists, we can help clients get in touch with this source. If the spiritual has created trauma and bad experiences, we can help clients find new healing paths.

"CAN I MENTION IT HERE?"

We will conclude this book with a client called Lisbeth. She and her family have needed various kinds of help for many years, but only recently did she meet a therapist where she could include her spiritual life in a helpful way. She says that she is absolutely certain that including the spiritual life of clients makes therapy so much better. She explains:

> *You know humans are much more than the physical body, much more than their own psychology. I felt I got a response at every level. Of course the practical things, how to live life with a violent husband and two children, that was the main emphasis, but the spiritual dimension or the spiritual openness was always there, so I became completely relaxed and completely natural with myself.*

Lisbeth says that her therapist has asked her questions such as: Does your spirituality grow during these times? Do you feel spiritually broken? Why do you think it happens? Do you think it has something to do with God?

However, Lisbeth points out that in addition to the family therapist, she feels forced by the system to see a psychologist. In that therapy, the spiritual dimension is not included, and she feels it does not touch her deeply. Considering her history and family context, it would be unnatural to leave this dimension out.

An interesting aspect is that the family therapist has helped Lisbeth find more balance with her different perspectives in life. Lisbeth says that the therapist believed that the spiritual aspect took up too much space in her life, and that she needed to take better care of her body:

Because she said, "Lisbeth, … you pay so much attention to the spiritual, I think the spiritual is very important in life but you must put more emphasis on your body and the physical part".

Lisbeth agrees entirely with the family therapist; the connection between the physical, the psychological and the spiritual is very important. What she also knows is that these aspects are part of therapists as well.

Lisbeth feels acknowledged and welcomed in the systemic dialogue; it goes into her resources and language, and she feels that she can tell it like it is.

"Can I mention it here?" Lisbeth asked.

Hopefully, in your practice—you can say yes!

Reflections

1. You have now reached the end of the book. Has anything changed since you started reading?
2. Did you learn something new by reading the book? What do you feel is important?
3. Concerning the book's theme; What do you want to learn more about?

References

Arman, M., Alvenäng, A., El Madani, N., Hammarqvist, A.-S., & Ranheim, A. (2013). Caregiving for existential wellbeing: existential literacy. A clinical study in an anthroposophic healthcare context. *Ipdj International Practice Development Journal, 3*(1), 1–15.

Haram, A. (2004). *Dialogens kraft: når tanker blir stemmer (The power of dialogue. When thoughts become voices.).* Universitetsforl.

Telfener, U. (2017). Becoming through Belonging: The Spiritual Dimension in Psychotherapy. *Australian and New Zealand Journal of Family Therapy*, *38*(1), 156–167. https://doi.org/10.1002/anzf.1199

Yalom, I. D. (2015). *Creatures of a day: and other tales of psychotherapy*. Basic Books.

REFERENCES

Adams, N. (1995). Spirituality, science and therapy. *Australian and New Zealand Journal of Family Therapy, 16*(4), 201–208.

Akerhaug, L. (2008). *Jøder—ikke bare jøder*. Forskning.no.

Antonovsky, A. (1987). *Unraveling the mystery of health: how people manage stress and stay well*. Jossey-Bass.

Aponte, H. J. (2002). Spirituality: The heart of therapy. In T. D. Carlson, Erickson, M.J. (Ed.), *Spirituality and Family Therapy*. Routledge.

Aponte, H. J. (2009). The stress of povertry and the comfort of spirituality. In F. Walsh (Ed.), *Spiritual resourses in family therapy* (2 ed., pp. 125–140). The Guliford Press.

Arman, M., Alvenäng, A., El Madani, N., Hammarqvist, A.-S., & Ranheim, A. (2013). Caregiving for existential wellbeing: existential literacy. A clinical study in an anthroposophic healthcare context. *Ipdj International Practice Development Journal, 3*(1), 1–15.

Balmer, T. D., Van Asselt, K. W., Walker, C., & Kennedy, B. R. (2012). A Phenomenological Study of Spiritual Values in Secular-Based Marriage and Family Therapists [Article]. *Journal of spirituality in mental health, 14*(4), 242–258. https://doi.org/10.1080/19349637.2012.730466

Banmen, J., & Maki-Banmen, K. (2014). What Has Become of Virginia Satir's Therapy Model Since She Left Us in 1988? *Journal of Family Psychotherapy, 25*(2), 117–131.

Barker, S., & Scammell, J. (2016). *Psychology for nursing and healthcare professionals: developing compassionate care*. Sage.

Bateson, G. (1979). *Mind and nature: a necessary unity*. Wildwood House.
Bateson, G. (2000). *Steps to an ecology of mind*. University of Chicago Press.
Bateson, G., & Bateson, M. C. (1987a). *Angels fear: towards an epistemology of the sacred*. Macmillan.
Bateson, G., & Bateson, M. C. (1987b). *Angels fear: towards an epistemology of the sacred*. Macmillan.
Bateson, G., & Bateson, M. C. (2005). *Angels fear: towards an epistemology of the sacred*. Hampton press.
Benner, D. G. (2011). *Soulful spirituality: becoming fully alive and deeply human*. Brazos Press.
Benner, D. G. (2016). *Human being and becoming: living the adventure of life and love*. Brazos Press, a division of Baker Publishing Group.
Berry, T. (2009). *The sacred universe: earth, spirituality, and religion in the twenty-first century*. Columbia University Press.
Berry, T., Tucker, M. E., & Grim, J. (2014). *Selected writings on the earth community*. Orbis Books.
Bidwell, D. E. (2016). *Spirituality, Social Construction and Relational Processes: Essays and Reflections*. A Tao Institute Publication.
Binder, P.-E. (2022). Suffering a Healthy Life-On the Existential Dimension of Health. *Frontiers in psychology, 13*, 803792–803792.
Binder, P.-E. (2023). Eksistensiell psykoterapi. *Tidsskrift for Norsk psykologforening, 60*(12), 831–840. https://doi.org/10.52734/VFBM1057
Blair, L. J. (2015). The influence of therapists' spirituality on their practice: A grounded theory exploration. *Counselling and Psychotherapy Research, 15*(3), 161–170.
Blanton, P. G. (2005). Narrative Family Therapy and Spiritual Direction: Do They Fit? [Article]. *Journal of Psychology & Christianity, 24*(1), 68–79. http://search.ebscohost.com/login.aspx?direct=true&db=afh&AN=16802929&site=ehost-live
Borge, L., & Mæland, E. (2017). Er det rom for livssynstemaer i dagens psykisk helsearbeid? *Klinisk Sygepleje, 31*(03), 165–177. http://www.idunn.no/klinisk_sygepleje/2017/03/er_det_rom_for_livssynstemaer_idagens_psykisk_helsearbeid
Bowen, M. (1978). *Family therapy in clinical practice*. Aronson.
Brownell, P. (2015). *Spiritual competency in psychotherapy* (1st ed.). Springer Publishing Company.
Burnham, J. (2005). Relational reflexivity: a tool for socially constructing therapeutic relationships. *The space between: Experience, context and process in the therapeutic relationship*. London: Karnac.
Burnham, J. (2012). Developments in Social GRRRAAACCEEESSS: visible–invisible and voiced–unvoiced. *Culture and Reflexivity in Systemic Psychotherapy. Mutual Perspectives*, 139–160.

Burr, V. (2015). *Social constructionism*. Routledge.

Butler, M. H., & Harper, J. M. (1994). The divine triangle: God in the marital system of religious couples. *Family Process, 33*(3), 277–286.

Campbell, W., Tamasese, K., & Waldegrave, C. (2001). Just Therapy. In D. Denborough (Ed.), *Family Therapy: Exploring the filed's past, present & possible futures*. Dulwich Centre Publications.

Canda, E. R., & Furman, L. D. (2010). *Spiritual diversity in social work practice* (2nd ed.). Oxford University Press.

Capra, F., & Luisi, P. L. (2016). *Liv, system, helhed: det levende som system: en syntese*. Forlaget Mindspace.

Carlson, T., & Erickson, M. (2009). *Spirituality and Family Therapy*. Routledge.

Carlson, T., & Erickson, M. J. (2000). Re-authoring spiritual narratives: God in persons' relational identity stories. *Journal of Systemic Therapies, 19*(2), 65–83.

Carlson, T., McGeorge, C., & Anderson, A. (2011). The Importance of Spirituality in Couple and Family Therapy: A Comparative Study of Therapists' and Educators' Beliefs [Article]. *Contemporary Family Therapy: An International Journal, 33*(1), 3–16. https://doi.org/10.1007/s10591-010-9136-0

Carlson, T., McGeorge, C., & Toomey, R. (2014). Establishing the Validity of the Spirituality in Clinical Training Scale: Measuring the Level of Integration of Spirituality and Religion in Family Therapy Training [Article]. *Contemporary Family Therapy: An International Journal, 36*(2), 310–325. https://doi.org/10.1007/s10591-013-9278-y

Charmaz, K. (2014). *Constructing grounded theory* (2nd ed.). Sage.

Cook, C. C. H. (2004). Addiction and spirituality. *Addiction, 99*(5), 539–551. https://doi.org/10.1111/j.1360-0443.2004.00715.x

Corbett, L. (2011). *The Sacred Cauldron: psychotherapy as a spiritual practice*. Chiron.

Coyle, S. M. (2022a). Spirituality in Individual, Tandem, and Group Supervision. In *Spirituality in Systemic Family Therapy Supervision and Training* (pp. 73–93). Springer.

Coyle, S. M. (2022b). *Spirituality in Systemic Family Therapy Supervision and Training* (1 ed.). Cham: Springer International Publishing AG. https://doi.org/10.1007/978-3-030-92369-3

Dallos, R., & Vetere, A. (2021). *Systemic therapy and attachment narratives: Applications in a range of clinical settings*. Routledge.

Danbolt, L. J. (2014). *Religionspsykologi*. Gyldendal Akademisk.

DeMarinis, V. (2008). The impact of postmodernization on existential health in Sweden: Psychology of religion's function in existential public health analysis. *Archive for the Psychology of Religion, 30*(1), 57–74.

Deurzen, E. van & Iacovou, S. (2013). *Existential perspectives on relationship therapy*. Palgrave Macmillan.

Draper, B., & Green, H. (2020). *Soulful nature: a spiritual field guide*. Canterbury Press.

Drinkwater, K. G., Dagnall, N., Denovan, A., & Williams, C. (2021). Paranormal belief, thinking style and delusion formation: a latent profile analysis of within-individual variations in experience-based paranormal facets. *Frontiers in psychology, 12*, 670959.

Elkaïm, M. (1997). *If you love me, don't love me: undoing reciprocal double binds and other methods of change in couple and family therapy*. J. Aronson.

Elkins, D. N. (1999). *Beyond religion: a personal program for building a spiritual life outside the walls of traditional religion*. Quest Books, Theosophical Publ.

Engedal, L. G. (2004). Kristen sjelesorg i en postmoderne kultur: utfordringer og muligheter. In (pp. 19–72). Verbum.

Erickson, M. J., & Carlson, T. (2014). *Spirituality and family therapy*. Routledge.

Eriksen, T. H. (2021). *Små steder - store spørsmål: innføring i sosialantropologi* (4. utgave. ed.). Universitetsforlaget.

Eriksson, K., Lindström, U. Å., & Åbo akademi Institutionen för, v. (2003). *Gryning: II: Klinisk vårdvetenskap* (Vol. II). Institutionen för vårdvetenskap, Åbo Akademi.

Ernvik, U. (2022). *Ekopsykoterapi: psykoterapi i och med naturen för vuxna och barn* (Upplaga 1. ed.). Studentlitteratur.

Esmiol Wilson, E., & Nice, L. (2018). *Socially Just Religious and Spiritual Interventions: Ethical Uses of Therapeutic Power* (1st 2018. ed.). Cham: Springer International Publishing AG. https://doi.org/10.1007/978-3-030-01986-0

Falicov, C. J. (1995). Training to think culturally: A multidimensional comparative framework. *Family process, 34*(4), 373–388.

Frankl, V. E. (1992). *Man's search for meaning: an introduction to logotherapy* (4th ed.). Beacon Press.

Frankl, V. E. (2004). *Man's search for meaning: the classic tribute to hope from the Holocaust*. Rider.

Freire, P. (1979). *Pedagogy of the oppressed*. Sheed and Ward.

Fromm, E. (2006). *The art of loving* (Fiftieth anniversary ed.). Harper Perennial.

Geels, A., Wikström, O., Hermanson, J., & Junus, P. (2006). *Den religiösa människan: en introduktion till religionspsykologin* ([5. omarb. utg.]. ed.). Natur och Kultur.

Gergen, K. J. (1999). *An invitation to social construction*. Sage.

Gergen, K. J. (2009a). *An invitation to social construction* (2nd ed.). SAGE.

Gergen, K. J. (2009b). *Relational being: beyond self and community*. Oxford University Press.

Gockel, A. (2011). Client Perspectives on Spirituality in the Therapeutic Relationship [Article]. *Humanistic Psychologist, 39*(2), 154–168. https://doi.org/10.1080/08873267.2011.564959

Grams, W., Carlson, T., & McGeorge, C. (2007). Integrating Spirituality into Family Therapy Training: An Exploration of Faculty Members' Beliefs [Article]. *Contemporary Family Therapy: An International Journal, 29*(3), 147–161. https://doi.org/10.1007/s10591-007-9042-2

Griffith, B. A., & Rotter, J. C. (1999). Families and spirituality: Therapists as facilitators. *The Family Journal, 7*(2), 161–164.

Group, W. S. (2006). A cross-cultural study of spirituality, religion, and personal beliefs as components of quality of life. *Social science & medicine (1982), 62*(6), 1486–1497. https://doi.org/10.1016/j.socscimed.2005.08.001

Grover, T., Myra, S. M., & Axberg, U. (2023). *New Horizons in Systemic Practice with Adults* (1 ed.). Cham: Springer International Publishing AG. https://doi.org/10.1007/978-3-031-30526-9

Habermas, J. (2008). Notes on a post-secular society. *Revista colombiana de sociología* (31), 169–183.

Haram, A. (2004). *Dialogens kraft: når tanker blir stemmer (The power of dialogue. When thoughts become voices.)*. Universitetsforl.

Harris, S. M. (1998). Finding a forest among trees: Spirituality hiding in family therapy theories. *Journal of Family Studies, 4*(1), 77–86.

Haug, I. (1998a). Including a spiritual dimension in family therapy: Ethical considerations. *Contemporary family therapy, 20*(2), 181–194.

Haug, I. (1998b). Spirituality as a Dimension of Family Therapists' Clinical Training. *Contemporary family therapy, 20*(4), 471–483. https://doi.org/10.1023/A:1021628132514

Heelas, P. (2008). *Spiritualities of life: New Age romanticism and consumptive capitalism.* Blackwell Publ.

Hegel, G. W. (1977). *Phenomenology of spirit.* Oxford University Press.

Heidegger, M. (1982). *On the way to language.* HarperOne.

Helminiak, D. A. (2001). Treating Spiritual Issues in Secular Psychotherapy [Article]. *Counseling & Values, 45*(3), 163. http://search.ebscohost.com/login.aspx?direct=true&db=afh&AN=4427875&site=ehost-live

Hill, P. C., & Pargament, K. I. (2003). Advances in the conceptualization and measurement of religion and spirituality. Implications for physical and mental health research. *Am Psychol, 58*(1), 64–74.

Hodge, D. R. (2005). Spiritual assessment in marital and family therapy: A methodological framework for selecting from among six qualitative assessment tools. *Journal of marital and Family Therapy, 31*(4), 341–356.

Hodge, D. R., & Horvath, V. E. (2011). Spiritual Needs in Health Care Settings: A Qualitative Meta-Synthesis of Clients' Perspectives [Article]. *Social Work, 56*(4), 306–316. http://search.ebscohost.com/login.aspx?direct=true&db=afh&AN=69822099&site=ehost-live

Holm, C. C., Karlsson, B. E., & Holmberg, Å. (2023). Experiences of spirituality of in- and out-patients in mental health facilities: A thematic synthesis of qualitative studies. *Journal of spirituality in mental health, ahead-of-print*(ahead-of-print), 1–30. https://doi.org/10.1080/19349637.2023.2213455

Holmberg, Å. (2012). Familieterapeuters møte med det åndelige og eksistensielle mennesket. *Fokus på familien, 40*(01), 49–66.

Holmberg, Å. (2018). *Making room for spirituality?: family therapists' and clients' perceptions and experiences about spirituality in family therapy* VID Specialized University]. Oslo.

Holmberg, Å., & Carlsson, B. (2023). Givin resonans and room to spirituality in systemic practice. In T. Grøver, S. M. Myra, & U. Axberg (Eds.), *New Horizons in Systemic Practice with Adults* (pp. 81–96). Palgrave Macmillan.

Holmberg, Å., & Jensen, P. (2024). Spirituality: A meaningful philosophy of life and a "lifeline" in times of crises. In (1 ed., Vol. 1, pp. 122–132). Routledge. https://doi.org/10.4324/9781003308096-13

Holmberg, Å., Jensen, P., & Ulland, D. (2017). To Make Room or Not to Make Room: Clients' Narratives About Exclusion and Inclusion of Spirituality in Family Therapy Practice. *Australian and New Zealand Journal of Family Therapy, 38*(1), 15–26. https://doi.org/10.1002/anzf.1198

Holmberg, Å., Jensen, P., & Vetere, A. (2021). Spirituality–a forgotten dimension? Developing spiritual literacy in family therapy practice. *Journal of Family Therapy, 43*(1), 78–95.

Holmberg, Å., & Karlsson, B. (2023). Giving Resonance and Room to Spirituality in Systemic Practice. In (pp. 81–96). Cham: Springer International Publishing. https://doi.org/10.1007/978-3-031-30526-9_6

Honneth, A. (1995). *The struggle for recognition: the moral grammar of social conflicts*. Polity Press.

Hoogestraat, T., & Trammel, J. (2003). Spiritual and Religious Discussions in Family Therapy: Activities to Promote Dialogue [Article]. *American Journal of Family Therapy, 31*(5), 413. https://doi.org/10.1080/01926180390224049

Jamison, C. (2022). *Finding the language of grace*. Bloomsbury Publishing Plc.

Jandt, F. E. (1995). *Intercultural communication: an introduction*. Sage.

Janis, S. (2008). *Spirituality for dummies*. Wiley Publishing Inc.

Jenkinson, S. (2015). *Die wise: a manifesto for sanity and soul*. North Atlantic Books.

Jensen, P. (2008). *The Narratives which connect...: a qualitative research approach to the Narratives which connect therapists' personal and private lives to their family therapy practices*. University of East London]. London.

Jensen, P. (2012). Family Therapy, Personal Life and Therapeutic Practice. The Map of Relational Resonance as a Language for Analyzing Psychotherapeutic Processes. *Human Systems: The Journal of Therapy, Consultation & Training, 23*(1), 68–87.

Jeong Woong, C., & Canda, E. R. (2010). The Meaning and Engagement of Spirituality for Positive Youth Development in Social Work [Article]. *Families in Society, 91*(2), 121–126. https://doi.org/10.1606/1044-3894.3981

Johannessen, E. (2007). *Mye er forskjellig - men bare utenpå?: om barn, barneopp-dragelse og utdanning i en mangfoldig verden.* Sebu forl.

Johannessen, Ø. L. (2006). Coping with cultural encounters in education. In (pp. s. 171–183). Unipub forl./Oslo Academic Press.

Jørgensen, H., & van der Weele, J. (2009). Vold i storfamiliekontekst–erfaringer fra Alternativ til Vold. *Eide, NA Qureshi, M. Rugkåsa & H. Vike (Red.), Over profesjonelle barrierer. Et minoritetsperspektiv i psykososialt arbeid med barn og unge.* Oslo: Gyldendal Akademisk.

Jung, C. G. (1966). *Psychology and religion.* Yale University Press.

Kaur, V. (2020). *See no stranger: a memoir and manifesto of revolutionary love* (First edition.). One World.

Khan, N. (2022). A qualitative exploration of systemic training and practice for Muslim community leaders as part of an innovative project in an inner-city area. *Journal of Family Therapy, 44*(1), 124–141.

Koca, D. A. (2017). Spirituality-based analysis of Satir family therapy. *Spiritual Psychology and Counseling, 2*(2), 121–142.

Koenig, King D. E., & Carson, V. B. (2012). *Handbook of religion and health* (2nd ed.). Oxford University Press.

la Cour, P., Ausker, N. H., & Hvidt, N. C. (2012). Six Understandings of the Word 'Spirituality' in a Secular Country. *Archive for the Psychology of Religion, 34*(1), 63–81. https://doi.org/10.1163/157361212X649634

Lagerkvist, P. (1959). *Sibyllan.* Bonnier.

Lantz, J. (1994a). Mystery in family therapy. *Contemporary family therapy, 16*(1), 53–66.

Lantz, J. (1994b). Primary and secondary reflection in existential family therapy. *Contemporary family therapy, 16*(4), 315–327.

Larner, G. (2017). Spiritual Dialogues in Family Therapy. *Australian and New Zealand Journal of Family Therapy, 38*(1), 125–141. https.//doi.org/10.1002/anzf.1207

Laugerud, T. (2012). Kirken i møte med åndelige erfaringer i grenseland til kristen tro. *Tidsskrift for praktisk teologi, 1.*

Lloyd, C. (2018). *Moments of meaning–Towards an assessment of protective and risk factors for existential vulnerability among young women with mental ill-health concerns: A mixed methods project in clinical psychology of religion and existential health* Acta Universitatis Upsaliensis].

Luke, A. (2012). Critical literacy: Foundational notes. *Theory into practice, 51*(1), 4–11.

Lukoff, D., Turner, R., & Lu, F. (1992). Transpersonal psychology research review: Psychoreligious dimensions of healing. *The Journal of Transpersonal Psychology, 24*(1), 41.

Lum, W. (2002). The use of self of the therapist. *Contemporary family therapy, 24*(1), 181–197.

Lundsbye, M. (2010). *Familjeterapins grunder: ett interaktionistiskt perspektiv, baserat på system-, process- och kommunikationsteori.* Natur och Kultur.

Magaldi-Dopman, D., Park-Taylor, J., & Ponterotto, J. G. (2011). Psychotherapists' spiritual, religious, atheist or agnostic identity and their practice of psychotherapy: a grounded theory study. *Psychother Res, 21*(3), 286–303. https://doi.org/10.1080/10503307.2011.565488

Malkomsen, A., & Malkomsen, A. (2023). *Hva er poenget?: om meningsløshetens psykologi og eksistensielle samtaler* (1. utgave. ed.). Fagbokforlaget.

Martinez, K. J. (1994). Cultural sensitivity in family therapy gone awry. *Hispanic Journal of Behavioral Sciences, 16*(1), 75–89.

Maturana, H. R., & Varela, F. J. (1992). *The tree of knowledge: the biological roots of human understanding* (Rev. ed.). Shambhala.

McGilchrist, I. (2021). *The matter with things: our brains, our delusions and the unmaking of the world.* Perspectiva Press.

McLaren, B. D. (2016). *The Great Spiritual Migration: How the World's Largest Religion Is Seeking a Better Way to Be Christian.* The Crown Publishing Group.

McNeil, S., Pavkov, T., Hecker, L., & Killmer, J. (2012). Marriage and Family Therapy Graduate Students' Satisfaction with Training Regarding Religion and Spirituality [Article]. *Contemporary Family Therapy: An International Journal, 34*(4), 468–480. https://doi.org/10.1007/s10591-012-9205-7

Merleau-Ponty, M. (1962). *Phenomenology of perception.* Routledge.

Merleau-Ponty, M. (2012). Phenomenology of perception. In. Routledge.

Miller McInnes, M., & Van Ness Sheppard, N. (2014). What Does Spirituality Mean to You? Mapping the Spiritual Discourses of Psychotherapy Graduate Students. *Journal of spirituality in mental health, 16*(4), 286–310. https://doi.org/10.1080/19349637.2014.957605

Miller, W. R., & Thoresen, C. E. (2003). Spirituality, religion, and health. An emerging research field. *Am Psychol, 58*(1), 24–35.

Moore, T. (1992). *Care of the soul: a guide for cultivating depth and sacredness in everyday life.* HarperCollins.

Myskja, A. (2015). *Helbred dig selv: styrk din egen modstandskraft* (p. 213). Klim.

Neden, J., Barber, J., Bradbury, G., & Cheung, A. (2011). Bringing forth spirituality dialogues in family therapy education [Article]. *Journal of Family Therapy, 33*(2), 224–228. https://doi.org/10.1111/j.1467-6427.2011.00532.x

Nordhelle, G., & Sakhi, U. S. (2019). *Angstens røtter: eksistensiell forståelse og mestring.* Fagbokforlaget.

Næss, A., & Haukeland, P. I. (2008). *Life's philosophy: reason & feeling in a deeper world.* University of Georgia Press.

Olsen, H. (2006). *Spiritualitet: en ny dimensjon i religionsforskningen* (Vol. nr 127). Høgskolen i Agder.

Paloutzian, R. F., & Park, C. L. (2013). *Handbook of the psychology of religion and spirituality* (2nd ed.). Guilford Press.

Pargament, K. I. (2007). *Spiritually integrated psychotherapy: understanding and addressing the sacred.* Guilford Press.

Patterson, J., Hayworth, M., Turner, C., & Raskin, M. (2000). SPIRITUAL ISSUES IN FAMILY THERAPY: A GRADUATE-LEVEL COURSE [Article]. *Journal of Marital & Family Therapy, 26*(2), 199–210. http://ezproxy.diastud.no/login?url=http://search.ebscohost.com/login.aspx?direct=true&db=afh&AN=3582013&site=ehost-live

Pearson, A. (2017). Working with Religious and Spiritual Experience in Family Therapy: Manna for the Journey. *Australian and New Zealand Journal of Family Therapy, 38*(1), 43–60. https://doi.org/10.1002/anzf.1202

Piltz, A. (1991). *Mellan ängel och best: människans värdighet och gåta i europeisk tradition.* Alfabeta.

Plotkin, B. (2003). *Soulcraft: Crossing into the Mysteries of Nature and Psyche.* New World Library.

Post, B. C., & Wade, N. G. (2009). Religion and spirituality in psychotherapy: a practice-friendly review of research [Article]. *Journal of Clinical Psychology, 65*(2), 131–146. http://search.ebscohost.com/login.aspx?direct=true&db=afh&AN=36078396&site=ehost-live

Qureshi, N. A. (2009). Kultursensitivitet i profesjonell yrkesutøvelse. In (pp. 206–230). Gyldendal akademisk.

Reed, E. S. (1998). *From soul to mind: The emergence of psychology from Erasmus Darwin to William James.* Yale University Press.

Rizzutto, A.-M. (2009). Psychoanalytic considerations about spiritually oriented psychotherapy In L. Sperry & E. P. Shafranske (Eds.), *Spiritually oriented psychotherapy* (pp. 31–50). American Psychological Association.

Roach, M. (2003). *Stiff: the curious lives of human cadavers* (Large print ed.). Thorndike Press.

Rober, P. (2005). The Therapist's Self in Dialogical Family Therapy: Some Ideas About Not-Knowing and the Therapist's Inner Conversation. *Family Process, 44*(4), 477–495. https://doi.org/10.1111/j.1545-5300.2005.00073.x

Robinson, M., Robinson, M., & Jordal, P. (2023). *Hva gjør vi her?: en essaysamling om litteratur, språk og teologi.* Verbum.

Rogers, M. E. (1970). *An introduction to the theoretical basis of nursing.* F. A. Davis.

Rogoff, B. (2003). *The cultural nature of human development* (1st ed.). Oxford University Press.

Rohr, R. (2011). *Falling upward: a spirituality for the two halves of life.* Jossey-Bass.

Rohr, R. (2013). *Immortal diamond: the search for our true self.* SPCK.

Rohr, R. (2014). *Eager to love: the alternative way of Francis of Assisi.* Franciscan Media.

Rohr, R. (2018). *Richard Rohr: essential teachings on love.* ORBIS books.

Rohr, R. (2019). *The universal Christ: how a forgotten reality can change everything we see, hope for and believe.* SPCK, Society for Promoting Christian Knowledge; Convergent Books.

Rohr, R. (2021). *Breathing under Water: Spirituality and the Twelve Steps.* Franciscan Media.

Rohr, R., & Chase, J. (2018). *Richard Rohr: essential teachings on love.* ORBIS.

Rosa, H. (2019). *Resonance: a sociology of our relationship to the world.* Polity.

Saint-Jean, P. (2022). *The crucible of racism: Ignatian spirituality and the power of hope.* Orbis Books.

Sakhi, U. S., & Nordhelle, G. (2021). *Å leve i pakt med Moder jord: integral terapi* (1. utgave. ed.). Cappelen Damm.

Satir, V. (1988). *The new peoplemaking.* Science and Behavior Books.

Satir, V. (1991). *The Satir model: family therapy and beyond.* Science and Behavior Books.

Schibbye, A.-L. L. (2006). *Livsbevissthet: om å være til stede i eget liv.* Universitetsforl.

Schibbye, A.-L. L. (2009). *Relasjoner: et dialektisk perspektiv på eksistensiell og psykodynamisk psykoterapi* (2. utg. ed.). Universitetsforl.

Seikkula, J. (2008). Inner and outer voices in the present moment of family and network therapy. *Journal of Family Therapy, 30*(4), 478–491. https://doi.org/10.1111/j.1467-6427.2008.00439.x

Serrander, E. (2018). När kroppen visar vägen. In D. Stiwne (Ed.), *Existens och psykisk hälsa* (pp. 65–87). Studentlitteratur.

Sheehan, J., Flaskas, C., & McCarthy, I. (2007). *Hope and despair in narrative and family therapy: adversity, forgiveness, and reconciliation.* Routledge.

Sheldrake, P. (2007). *A brief history of spirituality.* Blackwell Publ.

Shorter, E. (1977). *The making of the modern family.* Fontana.

Shorter, E. (1979). *Kernefamiliens historie.* Nyt nordisk forlag.

Sinclair, S., & Chochinov, H. M. (2012). Communicating with patients about existential and spiritual issues: SACR-D work. *Progress in Palliative Care, 20*(2), 72–78. https://doi.org/10.1179/1743291X12Y.0000000015

Stiwne, D. (2018). *Existens och psykisk hälsa: om hur liv och levnad förhåller sig till hälsa och ohälsa.* Studentlitteratur.

Stripp, T. A., Wehberg, S., Büssing, A., Koenig, H. G., Balboni, T. A., VanderWeele, T. J., Søndergaard, J., & Hvidt, N. C. (2023). Spiritual needs in Denmark: a population-based cross-sectional survey linked to Danish national registers. *The Lancet Regional Health–Europe, 28.*

Swinton, J. (2001). *Spiritual and mental health care. Rediscovering a forgotten dimension.* Jessica Kingsley Publisher.

Swinton, J. (2020). *Finding Jesus in the storm: the spiritual lives of Christians with mental health challenges.* William. B. Eerdmans Publishing Company.

Telfener, U. (2017). Becoming through Belonging: The Spiritual Dimension in Psychotherapy. *Australian and New Zealand Journal of Family Therapy, 38*(1), 156–167. https://doi.org/10.1002/anzf.1199

Thayne, T. R. (1998). Opening space for clients' religious and spiritual values in therapy: A social constructionist perspective. *Journal of Family Social Work, 2*(4), 13–23.

Trimble, D. (2018). *Engaging with Spirituality in Family Therapy: Meeting in Sacred Space* (1st 2018. ed.). Cham: Springer International Publishing AG. https://doi.org/10.1007/978-3-319-77410-7

Tønder, E. S., & Karlsson, B. E. (2020). Resonans i relasjoner (Resonance in relations). In N. Buus, B. Askham, & L. L. Berring (Eds.), *Psykiatrisk sykepleje* (pp. 375–398). Munksgaard. (Reprinted from 2nd.)

Ulland, D. (2012). Embodied spirituality. https://doi.org/10.116 3/157361212X645340

Ulland, D., & DeMarinis, V. (2014). Understanding and working with existential information in a Norwegian adolescent psychiatry context: a need and a challenge [Article]. *Mental Health, Religion & Culture, 17*(6), 582–593. https://doi.org/10.1080/13674676.2013.871241

van Deurzen, E. (2003). 13 Existentialism and existential psychotherapy. *Heart and Soul: The Therapeutic Face of Philosophy*, 216.

Vetere, A. (2023). We cannot find peace in restlessness. How the neuroscience supports psychotherapeutic practice. *Human Systems*, 26344041231203378.

Vike, H., & Eide, K. (2009). Kulturanalyse, minoritetsperspektiv og psykososialt arbeid. In (pp. s. 13–37). Gyldendal akademisk.

Waldegrave, C. (2003). Grappling with a contemporary and inclusive spirituality. *Just Therapy–a Journey: A Collection of Papers from the Just Therapy Team* New Zealand Adelaide: Dulwich Centre Publications.

Walsh, F. (1999). *Spiritual resources in family therapy*. Guilford Press.

Walsh, F. (2003). *Normal family process: Growing diversity and complexity* (2nd ed.). Guilford Press.

Walsh, F. (2009a). Religion, spirituality, and the family: Multifaith Perspectives. In F. Walsh (Ed.), *Spiritual resources in family therapy* (2 ed., pp. 3–30). The Guildford Press.

Walsh, F. (2009b). *Spiritual resources in family therapy*. Guilford Press.

Walsh, F. (2010). Spiritual Diversity: Multifaith Perspectives in Family Therapy [Article]. *Family Process, 49*(3), 330–348. https://doi.org/10.1111/j.1545-5300.2010.01326.x

Walsh, F. (2012a). *Normal family processes: growing diversity and complexity* (4th ed.). Guilford Press.

Walsh, F. (2012b). *Normal family processes: Growing diversity and complexity.* Guilford Press.

Walsh, F. (2013). Religion and spirituality: A family systems perspective in clinical practice. In K. I. Pargament, A. Mahoney, & E. P. Shafranske (Eds.), *APA Handbook of Psychology, Religion and Spirituality* (Vol. 2, pp. 189–205). American Psychological Association.

Wampold, B. E., & Imel, Z. E. (2015). *The great psychotherapy debate; The Evidence for What Makes Psychotherapy Work.* Routledge.

Wendel, R. (2003). Lived Religion and Family Therapy: What Does Spirituality Have to Do with It? [Article]. *Family Process*, 42(1), 165. http://search.ebsco-host.com/login.aspx?direct=true&db=afh&AN=9407479&site=ehost-live

Wickström, O. (2007). *Det bländande mörkret. Att upptäcka den stora glädjen*. Libris.

Worthington, E. L., & Sandage, S. J. (2016). *Forgiveness and spirituality in psychotherapy: A relational approach*. American Psychological Association. https://doi.org/10.1037/14712-000

Yalom, I. D. (2015). *Creatures of a day: and other tales of psychotherapy*. Basic Books.

Zaman, K. (1999). *Norge i svart, hvitt og brunt: en multikulturell mosaikk*. Forum Aschehoug.

Øiestad, G. (2009). *Selvfølelsen*. Gyldendal.

Aadnanes, P. M. (2012). *Livssyn* (4. utg. ed.). Universitetsforl.

Aasen, J. (2012). *Flerkulturell pedagogikk: en innføring* (Rev. utg. ed.). Oplandske bokforl.

INDEX

The manufacturer's authorised representative in the EU is Springer
Nature Customer Service Centre GmbH, Europaplatz 3, 69115 Heidelberg,
Germany. If you have any concerns regarding our products, please
contact ProductSafety@springernature.com

Printed and bound by CPI Group (UK) Ltd, Croydon, CR0 4YY
24/04/2026
02096375-0001